D0073121

POLITICS
IN THE
AFRICAN-AMERICAN
NOVEL

POLITICS IN THE AFRICAN-AMERICAN NOVEL

James Weldon Johnson, W.E.B. Du Bois, Richard Wright, and Ralph Ellison

RICHARD KOSTELANETZ

Contributions in Afro-American and
African Studies, Number 143
Henry Louis Gates, Jr., Series Editor

GREENWOOD PRESS
New York • Westport, Connecticut • London

Especially for
Ralph W. and Fanny McConnell Ellison
John P. and Claudia Burghardt Morgan

PS374
P6
K67
1991

Library of Congress Cataloging-in-Publication Data

Kostelanetz, Richard.
    Politics in the African-American novel : James Weldon Johnson,
  W.E.B. Du Bois, Richard Wright, and Ralph Ellison / Richard
  Kostelanetz.
        p. cm. — (Contributions in Afro-American and African
  studies, ISSN 0069-9624 ; no. 143)
    Includes bibliographical references and index.
    ISBN 0-313-27471-1 (alk. paper)
    1. Political fiction, American—History and criticism.
  2. American fiction—Afro-American authors—History and criticism.
  3. Johnson, James Weldon, 1871-1938—Political and social views.
  4. Du Bois, W.E.B. (William Edward Burghardt), 1868-1963—
  Political and social views. 5. Wright, Richard, 1908-1960—
  Political and social views. 6. Ellison, Ralph—Political and
  social views. 7. Afro-Americans in literature. I. Title.
  II. Series.
  PS374.P6K67   1991
  810.9′358—dc20   90-19912

British Library Cataloguing in Publication Data is available.

Copyright © 1991 by Richard Kostelanetz

Library of Congress Catalog Card Number: 90-19912
ISBN: 0-313-27471-1
ISSN: 0069-9624

First published in 1991

Greenwood Press, 88 Post Road West, Westport, CT 06881
An imprint of Greenwood Publishing Group, Inc.

Printed in the United States of America

∞™

The paper used in this book complies with the
Permanent Paper Standard issued by the National
Information Standards Organization (Z39.48-1984).

10 9 8 7 6 5 4 3 2 1

Copyright Acknowledgments

Previous versions of these chapters appeared in *Negro-American Literature Forum, Xavier University Studies, Chicago Review, Commonweal, Twentieth Century,* and *Sewanee Review* where they were copyright © 1965, 1967, 1968, 1969 by Richard Kostelanetz. For permission to reprint extended passages of source quotations, I am grateful to Alfred A. Knopf for excerpts from *The Autobiography of an Ex-Colored Man* by James Weldon Johnson; to the Kraus Organization Limited for excerpts from *The Black Flame* (1957, 1959, 1961) by W.E.B. Du Bois; to Harper & Row for excerpts from several books by Richard Wright—*Native Son* (copyright 1940 by Richard Wright; © renewed 1968 by Ellen Wright); *Uncle Tom's Children* (copyright 1936; © renewed 1964 by Ellen Wright); *Black Boy* (copyright 1937, 1942, 1944, 1945); to Walker and Company for excerpts from *Lawd Today* by Richard Wright (copyright © 1963 by Ellen Wright); to Chatto & Windus for excerpts from *Eight Men* and *Lawd Today* by Richard Wright; to Jonathan Cape for excerpts from *Native Son* and *Black Boy* by Richard Wright; and to Random House for excerpts from *Invisible Man* by Ralph Ellison (copyright © 1952 by Ralph Ellison). Every effort has been made to verify the spelling of all proper names and to trace the ownership of all copyrighted material, in addition to making full acknowledgment of the latter's use. If any error or omission has occurred, it will be corrected in subsequent editions, providing that appropriate notification is submitted in writing to the author (P.O. Box 444, Prince St., New York, New York 10012). Every reasonable effort has been made to trace the owners of copyright materials in this book, but in some instances this has proven impossible. The publishers will be glad to receive information leading to more complete acknowledgments in subsequent printings of the book, and in the meantime extend their apologies for any omissions.

Epigraph

The resemblance between the historian and the novelist, to which I have already referred, here reaches its culmination. Each of them makes it his business to construct a picture which is partly narrative of events, partly a description of situations, exhibition of motives, analysis of characters. Each aims at making his picture a coherent whole, where every character and every situation is so bound up with the rest that his character in this situation cannot but act in this way, and we cannot imagine him as acting otherwise. The novel and the history must both of them make sense; nothing is admissible in either except what is necessary, and the judge of this necessity is in both cases the imagination. Both the novel and the history are self-explanatory, self-justifying, the product of an autonomous or self-authorizing activity; and in both cases, this activity is the *a priori* imagination.

—Robin G. Collinwood, *The Idea of History* (1956)

Let us take the case of the great Negro writer, Richard Wright. If we consider only his condition as a *man*, that is, as a Southern "nigger" transported to the North, we shall at once imagine that he can only write about Negroes or Whites *seen through the eyes of Negroes*. Can one imagine for a moment that he would agree to pass his life in the contemplation of the eternal True, Good, and

Beautiful when ninety percent of the Negroes in the South are practically deprived of the right to vote? And if anyone speaks here about the treason of the clerks, I answer that there are no clerks among the oppressed. Clerks are necessarily the parasites of oppressing classes or races. Thus, if an American Negro finds that he has a vocation as a writer, he discovers his subject at the same time. He is the man who sees the whites from the outside, who assimilates the white culture from the outside, and each of whose books will show the alienation of the black race within American society.

—Jean-Paul Sartre, "Why Write?" (1949)

I try to use an approach which is dictated not by my anger or my lack of anger, not by my protest or any lack of feelings of protest, but by the logic of the art itself. I write what my imagination throws up to me and I must feed this back through my own critical sensibility. That critical sensibility is informed by a sense of life which grows in its immediacy out of my being part of the Negro American group.

—Ralph Ellison, in an interview
with Richard Kostelanetz (1965)

I'm not a Negro leader. I have never thought of myself as a Negro leader. It is impossible to be a writer and a public spokesman. I'm a writer.

—James Baldwin, in an interview
with Dan Georgakis (1966)

Contents

Preface

More than any other literary form, the novel is obsessed with the impact of change upon personality. It was no mere historical accident that the novel came into prominence during the eighteenth century or that it became fully conscious of itself as an art form during the nineteenth. Its appearance marked the fulfillment of a social need that arose out of the accelerated process of historical change.

    —Ralph Ellison, "Society, Morality and the Novel" (1957)

The following chapter began as a thesis, "Politics in the Negro Novel in America," for the history department at Columbia University, which awarded me an M.A. degree in 1966. All chapters other than the introduction and conclusion appeared in journals in the late 1960s (that on James Weldon Johnson in the *Negro-American Literature Forum*, those on W.E.B. Du Bois and Richard Wright in *Xavier University Studies*, and that on Ralph Ellison in *Chicago Review*), and the Ellison chapter in particular has been frequently reprinted in critical anthologies about this work. I had always wanted to see the entire manuscript appear as a book, but not until Henry Louis (a.k.a. Skip) Gates asked to see it did that opportunity come. Thanks, Skip, and thanks as

well to Chip (a.k.a. Samuel R.) Delany, who graciously carried
the package to him.

On one hand, I had been interested in the literary representation
of history since doing an undergraduate independent study on
theories of history. On the other hand, in the summer of 1959,
at the end of the freshman year, Richard Foreman, then a college
friend, now a distinguished playwright, advised me to read Ralph
Ellison's *Invisible Man*, which struck me as an unusually rich
historical novel, to which I often returned in the ensuing years.
When I got to Columbia University, in American history (not
literature), I remember Professor Walter P. Metzger advising
our M.A. seminar that we should probably do our theses on a
minor historical figure who had not previously received scholarly
examination and that such research would inevitably involve
finding and reading this figure's personal papers. I panicked,
because, you see, then as now I have enormous difficulties
reading handwriting (including my own). The most convenient
alternative, I deduced, was to do something in intellectual history
that involved the interpretation of published texts; and since I was
in general more interested in literature and art than in political
history (and writers and artists more than politicians), it seemed
appropriate to work on the history of ideas in literature, which is
to say literature as reflective of intellectual history. Remembering
Invisible Man and believing as well in close analysis of literary
texts, I thought to see if I could read earlier novels for comparably
comprehensive interpretations of African-American politics.

This research was written up in 1965–1966, when I was living
in a low-income housing project on the edge of Harlem (our
Congressman was Adam Clayton Powell, while the folks in the
"middle-income" project across the street were represented by
William Fitts Ryan). I had already begun a literary career that
included reviews and articles, as well as British Broadcasting
Corporation film profiles of Ralph Ellison and Milton Babbitt; I
had been to London as a Fulbright scholar, this time in literature
rather than history. Nonetheless, it seemed important for me to
finish the thesis I had been researching, off and on, since the

early 1960s, and to get the degree that had been funded with fellowships from the Woodrow Wilson foundation and the New York State Regents, as well as a Columbia-only gift called an International Fellowship (to all of whom thanks again). Finish it I did, though often distracted to paralysis by the requirement of footnotes (which I have avoided in my writing ever since). Once accepted, this thesis was typed by Kenneth King, then a beginning dancer in New York, now a well-known choreographer and, like Richard Foreman, incidentally still a friend.

For publication now, the manuscript was retyped by me. Numerals appearing in parentheses directly after quotations from the novels refer to pages in the book discussed at that point; superscript numbers are notes to sources identified at the end of each chapter. Further documentation of these sources, such as editions used, appears in the bibliography concluding this book. I added an appendix of two essays also written at the time about figures and issues discussed in these pages.

Rereading (and retyping) the material now, I find myself impressed by the book's coherence, mostly because the novels could be read so neatly within my scheme, illustrating an operating assumption long clear to me—that a good idea can write a better thesis than a smart disorganized person (which is how I remember myself at the time). I remain as comfortable with its chronological structure, itself reflective of historical training, as well as with the close textual analysis in the tradition of modern literary criticism. Though generally resistant to anything resembling a fad, I have necessarily changed the adjectival epithet to conform with current usage, though at times earlier epithets appear, not only in my commentary but in quotations. I have read some scholarship written since about these writers and thought about incorporating their ideas, only to reject that option as destroying the coherence of the ancient text. (It was scarcely heartening to find that my earlier published work on these writers was rarely recognized, but as a veteran nonacademic I have become accustomed to second-class citizenship in the world of scholarship.) I thought of revising more; but unable to reconstruct the mind that wrote the thesis, I was unable to revise as much as I planned. I also thought about writing wholly new chapters on politics in the novels of younger African-American writers, such as William Melvin Kelley and Ishmael Reed; but as I could not do as well by these newer writers, I did not want to embarrass myself. Besides, I have a long-standing professional rule against doing anything that anyone else can do better, and it seems to me that other commentators, beginning with my friend Josef Jarab on Kelley and Reed himself on Reed, have already surpassed me. Blame on feckless youth the fact that the history included only familiar male writers; but since my approach was original in other ways, it was courageous enough for me to turn only the first stone.

I'm grateful to such current colleagues as professors Jerome Klinkowitz, Joe Johnson, and Charlotte Bonica for critically examining the present text prior to publication, and then to Dr. James Sabin and his colleagues at Greenwood Press for completing the reification process. The dedications acknowledge old friends, both sets of whom relate to the people in this book. Though I have since gone on to write much else, as well as work creatively in the new media, I did not find this text strange as I retyped it and so am pleased to see it finally appear as a book. Thanks to all who helped.

Richard Kostelanetz
New York, New York
14 May 1990

POLITICS
IN THE
AFRICAN-AMERICAN
NOVEL

one
_____

Introduction

> The meaning of American society and of the American situation
> to the Negro is summed up in such works as *Native Son, Invisible
> Man*, and *The Ordeal of Mansart*, and in two or three volumes
> of poetry . . . and the American Negro writer's entire spirit is
> represented by such writers as Richard Wright, Ralph Ellison,
> and William Burghardt Du Bois—by realists, surrealists, and
> romantic idealists.
>
> —Saunders Redding[1]

In suggesting that the historian resembles the novelist, in a
statement appearing as an epigraph to this book, the philosopher
Robin G. Collingwood implies an opposite thought—that the
novelist can function as an historian by portraying in fiction an
historical event to reveal its currents and causes; for even more
than the historian, the novelist endeavors to present a coherent
picture of an experience, which may just as feasibly be historical
as psychological or social.[2] In one crucial respect, however, the
historian and novelist differ: The historian generally deals with
specific historical events, admitting to his web of narrative
and explanation only facts that can be verified. Collingwood
added, "The historian's picture is meant to be true." However,
the novelist who treats history will portray, often subjectively,

larger, more encompassing developments, often so buried beneath the surface of experience that they cannot possibly be checked, for the novelist's purpose is presenting more general, more broadly conceived historical interpretations that are inevitably less verifiable. Therefore, in contrast to the historian who customarily intends to establish the definitive summary and analysis of a specific time-bound event or a series of events, the historical novelist will look at history to draw meanings of more universal, timeless implication: such concerns as the nature of man in society, the drift of history itself, the impact of history upon the individual, the relationship between the leader and his or her followers, and modes of historical understanding.

Leo Tolstoy's *War and Peace* (1868), to many minds the greatest of all historical novels, portrays a specific series of historical events but employs fictional techniques for a less specific truth. Although the novel is filled with verifiable details that reflect prodigious research, Tolstoy shapes his story, often creating scenes whole cloth, to illustrate relentlessly a certain thesis about the insignificance not only of Napolean but of all leaders—what Sir Isaiah Berlin calls "one of [Tolstoy's] celebrated paradoxes."

> The higher soldiers or statesmen are in the pyramid of author-ity, the farther they must be from its base which consists of those ordinary men and women whose lives are the actual stuff of history; and consequently, the smaller the effect of the words and acts of such remote personages, despite all their theoretical authority upon that history.[3]

In other words, Tolstoy was interpreting not only the Battle of Borodino but all battles, for all time. Other novelists have been more modest in their historical comments, focusing upon just, for example, the history of a people at a certain time, such as John Dos Passos's trilogy *U.S.A.* (1930–1936) or William Faulkner's *Absalom, Absalom* (1936), or the dynamics of a certain event or personage, such as Pocahontas's encounter with John Smith in

John Barth's *The Sot-Weed Factor* (1960) or Huey Long's career in Robert Penn Warren's *All the King's Men* (1946), or, with philosophical projection nearly equal to Tolstoy's, the meaning of history in our time, such as Thomas Pynchon's *V* (1963).[4] In short, the historical novelist at his or her best attempts to depict not the objective truth of pure historical scholarship but the subjective truth implicit in an overarching perception of history's general trend or meaning.

Of all native writers, African-American novelists in particular have frequently used fiction as an instrument for treating the historical experiences of their race; for not only have they commented upon the past and analyzed causes for success or failure but these novelists have also suggested the most viable future action for American blacks. African-American novelists have confronted this central political question: How can their people best achieve an optimal human existence—cultural, social, material, moral—in America? Every black person answers this question, at least implicitly, by the way he or she conducts his or her life; but not every change he or she makes to define or improve his or her lot is necessarily a political one. A political choice is one that implies *change through group action*, even though the choice may at first affect only the chooser. For example, to decide to purchase a better grade of food is a choice an individual makes to better his individual existence. Similarly individual would be the choice to flout whites' social barriers in an unsystematic, impulsive way, as the black boxing champion Jack Johnson did.[5] In contrast, going underground, as the narrators in fiction by both Richard Wright and Ralph Ellison do, is to intentionally change one's relationship with the above-ground world, symbolically as well as physically; and if many Afro-Americans expatriated themselves underground they would have pursued a collective political decision—engineered a change in their situation as people to a larger society. So, any individual action in a novel that implies a group action can be interpreted as embodying a political meaning. Although some political novelists, like Tolstoy in *War and Peace* or Dostoevsky in *The Possessed* (1872), attempt to depict the broad cloth of historical experience, most fiction writers choose to focus upon a single character or interrelated group, portraying them as confronting a political solution as an individual choice, yet making us aware that the individual choice epitomizes collective action. That is, these novelists resort to the common modern literary technique of making one man's experience stand for the encounters of the many—of creating a microcosm as a resonating symbol for the macrocosm.

Of course, not all African-American literature is political in subject or implication; in this respect, its fiction can be divided into three distinct groups. The first kind comes from authors who literarily "pass" for white, writing books indistinguishable from those written by white authors, using white characters and a prose that in no way reflects the race of its author. Frank Yerby, the Afro-American author of numerous popular romances of white Southern life, produces the most prominent examples of this kind of work. A lesser known example is Richard Wright's *Savage Holiday* (1954), which the black critic Arna Bontemps characterizes as "a paperback potboiler."[6] A book considerably better in quality, but similar in kind in this respect, is James Baldwin's *Giovanni's Room* (1956). The second group is primarily concerned with an Afro-American's problems with himself or herself and his or her community; they lack political resonance. Novels in this group range from sentimental books emphasizing local color, the characters' manners, and the author's mimicry to more serious works about, say, coming-of-age and intrafamilial disputes and relations. Typical of the former are Langston Hughes's stories about the character Simple. Two first-rate examples of the latter are James Baldwin's *Go Tell It on the Mountain* (1953) and Paule Marshall's *Brown Girl, Brownstones* (1959).

The third category contains novels that attempt to understand real predicaments in America, describing how Afro-Americans actually live, analyzing the forces that motivate their behavior and rule their lives. More often than not, these writers confront the prime Afro-American political questions, employing the novel as a conscious medium to understand and criticize the world around them. Indicatively, these novels are usually written by political men who, in addition to writing fiction, were active to varying degrees as spokesmen for and critics of their race; yet as serious writers each exhibited certain commitments to the task of creating excellence in imaginative literature.

This work in intellectual history will trace sequentially how Afro-American writers confront politics *in* their novels by analyzing political meanings in the works of four major figures—James Weldon Johnson (born 1871), W.E.B. Du Bois (born 1868), Richard Wright (born 1909), and Ralph Ellison (born 1914). In artistic achievement, their works are decidedly superior to the mass of fiction by Afro-Americans; and in their political implications, these novels embody attitudes fairly representative of each man's racial, intellectual contemporaries.[7] In the chapters that follow, each writer's fictional works will be treated in roughly chronological succession because the development of political ideas in literature is defined more by a series of novels than by biographies of authors working out their ideas in novels. This analytical strategy presumes that although a novel may influence political opinion and thus political leaders (the classic American example being Upton Sinclair's *The Jungle* [1906]), a political novel is more important for its truth-telling aims—for its analysis of history rather than its impact upon it. Unlike an expository work, which endeavors to describe and analyze, the novel, especially since the early nineteenth century and the age of critical realism, has endeavored to portray, either in direct or symbolic form, the truth of experience.[8] That is, novelistic art has become, in Stanley Edgar Hyman's phrase, "the only honest doctor who will tell us the truth."[9] The novelist whose intentions are polemical can have more of an impact by first offering a convincing portrayal of reality. For example, going underground might seem a frivolous notion if presented in an essay on "political alternatives for the African-Americans"; but a successful novelist, such as Ralph Ellison in *Invisible Man* (1952), can make it appear a viable choice for his narrator. In the end, then, this book is not about Afro-American political history but about the political novelists' responses to that political history, which is to say a facet of American intellectual history.

A "novel" can mean any form of imaginative prose work that is concerned with historically unspecific and/or embellished situations. Therefore, the autobiography of a representative black who emigrates from the South to a Northern city may be understood as essentially a fiction. An example is Richard Wright's *Black Boy* (1945), where the writer is also more concerned with shaping an imaginative whole, largely through the use of the techniques of fiction, than exhibiting a thoroughly scrupulous use of fact.[10] Similar fictional strategies shape Wright's 1944 memoir of his association with the American Communist Party (later included in Richard Crossman's *The God That Failed* [1949]). In contrast, the autobiography of a specific historical figure, acting in identifiable historical situations, must be classified as a variety of history; examples of Afro-American intellectual history include Frederick Douglass's autobiography (1882), W.E.B. Du Bois's *Autobiography* (1968), Martin Luther King's *Stride Toward Freedom* (1958), and Richard Wright's *Black Power* (1954).

The question of defining major political solutions is a knottier one, primarily because most of them arose as impromptu responses to particular situations rather than, as say Marxism did, a result of extensively premeditated thought.[11] Thus, Afro-American positions are less ideologies than ideas and attitudes that, aside from their intentions, may carry implications that are not immediately evident. Thus, too, these positions are not mutually exclusive, and many a black leader has been known to straddle two or more of them. The examples that follow, drawn from both novels and intellectual history, are themselves divided into two major groupings. For reasons that are largely historical and sociological, African-Americans in the North developed a different set of alternatives from their brethren in the South.

Historically, the usual fate for most of the black South, if not the likely fate for most of humankind's underdogs, was unresisting submission to existing authority. In post-Reconstruction times, such resignation to circumstance meant not only physical subservience to the economic slavery of agricultural and domestic labor but also, as the sociologist Gunnar Myrdal points out, tacit acceptance of the existing Southern black leadership who identified themselves by proximity to "quality folks, the best people among the whites," which is to say the white-dominated power structure. All alternatives to the status quo can be defined by their distance, both sociological and psychological, from this predominant submissive condition. A Southern social agency slightly removed from this position of subservience—more radical in spirit but hardly more effective in action—was the Commission on Interracial Cooperation, which was created by Southern white liberals. "One of its most important accomplishments," according to Myrdal, "is to have rendered interracial work socially respectable in the conservative South."[12] An Afro-American could learn to work within the white system, carving out for himself an existence that succeeded only as long as he seemed to obey white authority. On one level, this meant that he or she should cultivate skills to become a more desirable employee for the white community—this was Booker T. Washington's contribution to Afro-American thought; on another level, this strategy meant the development of an ironic attitude toward white authority, epitomized by the grandfather's advice to Ellison's narrator: "I want you to overcome 'em with yesses, undermine 'em with grins, agree 'em to death and destruction."[13] Afro-Americans who practiced this latter strategy believed it could afford or offer more true freedom of movement than outright recalcitrance; and as a measure of its typicality, the white literary critic Stanley Edgar Hyman, in the course of surveying Afro-American folk art and literature, perceived, "A smart man playing dumb . . . is a characteristic behavior pattern of Negroes in the South (and often in the North) in a variety of conflict situations."[14]

One step further along the spectrum is political rebellion, either to win more freedom within Southern society or to assume power over whites; and historically this tactic took several forms. First,

just after the Civil War, in some states there was the possibility of
legitimate political action, as blacks elected their own to state and
federal office.[15] However, the years between the Compromise of
1877 and Booker T. Washington's "The Atlanta Compromise"
of 1895 witnessed black disenfranchisement and disillusionment
with both the Republican party and orthodox political activity
in the South.[16] Only in recent years has official politics offered
blacks the possibility of access to governmental power. Another
form of rebellion, more successful nowadays, is nonviolent mass
action to redress grievances, to turn federal law into local custom,
and to initiate voter registration. Historically, this resistance
technique, borrowed from Mahatma Gandhi (who was influenced
in turn by Henry David Thoreau), was adapted to American
racial problems by the original Congress on Racial Equality
(CORE) in 1942; and although this group used nonviolent protest
sporadically throughout the North, it did not become a major
Southern strategy until Martin Luther King, Jr.'s Montgomery
Improvement Association used it in 1957. Since then, both King's
Southern Christian Leadership Conference and an offshoot of
King's movement, the Student Nonviolent Coordinating Committee, have made it their principal protest technique, with consider-
able success.[17]

The most radical form of rebellion within the South is black-
initiated counterviolence to avenge specific wrongs or to obtain
independence from white authority or intimidation. This tradition,
which dates back to the early slave revolts, had its most famous
exemplar in Nat Turner's rebellion of 1831.[18] Among the more
recent exponents within the South have been Robert Williams,
an N.A.A.C.P. official in North Carolina who, expelled from that
organization, has since emigrated to Cuba, and a newer group,
primarily from Louisiana, calling itself the Deacons.[19] Although
some researchers, particularly Herbert Aptheker, have attempted
to trace a continuity of revolt, most scholarship suggests that
rebellions were few and far between.[20] In fact, the alternative
of counterviolence has historically had few advocates within the
American South.

For most Southern blacks, the most viable form of revolt was rejection of the South itself, and nearly all expatriates took one of three paths. One direction led to the Midwest states and Southwestern territories, where Benjamin "Pap" Singleton, the self-styled "Moses of the colored exodus," thought that African-Americans could develop their own agriculture and industry in an atmosphere of independence within a system of segregation.[21] Although the Southwest had developed the liveliest black culture, as signified by the fact that nearly all the most imaginative jazz musicians came from there, and though it offered greater social opportunities, few Southern Afro-Americans moved there.[22] Another possibility was recolonization in Africa, a notion probably originated by Paul Cuffee in the late eighteenth century; but historically it generally earned more publicity than following.[23] The third choice was resettlement in the expanding urban areas of the North; and perhaps because this alternative offered the greatest economic incentive as well as less physical effort, it proved to be the most popular.[24] That accounts for why so many Afro-American novels portray emigration to the North.

However, for most African-Americans, the North hardly became a Nirvana, for there they found not equal social and economic opportunity but urban sludge, slum tenements, segregated housing, discrimination in employment, and a new kind of slavery:

> The Negro masses just sit at home in the ghetto amid the heat, the roaches, the rats, the vice, the disgrace, and rue the fact that come daylight they must meet the man—the white man—and work at a job that leads only to a dead end.[25]

The response to such conditions was again subservience—working within the existing industrial system, generally in jobs either too menial or dangerous to attract more employable, mobile whites, and therefore submitting to the system's vicissitudes of boom and bust. Although life in the North had its conspicuous pitfalls, all but a few Afro-Americans rejected the notion of returning South and looked instead toward other strategies. The least radical has been alliance with white-inspired, white-dominated and largely white-supported gradualist reform groups; and within this range falls the Urban League, which campaigns primarily for equal opportunity in obtaining jobs, and the National Association for the Advancement of Colored People (N.A.A.C.P.) which, along with its Legal Defense and Education Fund, looks primarily "upon the legal process as a weapon of social change," and upon "creating favorable publicity for the Negro people and winning a hearing for their grievances from the general American public." The major weaknesses of this position, historically, have been its political timidity on one hand and on the other, as Myrdal put it, "its lack of mass support." To put it differently, these groups finally hoped to influence what James Q. Wilson calls "politics in the narrower sense—the competitive struggle for elective office and deliberate attempts to influence the substance of government decisions."[26] In this respect, the activities of Representative Adam Clayton Powell are a direct extension of the Urban League and the N.A.A.C.P.

Similar in their Northern white origins and support and in their final ends, however different in means, are those more recent protest groups that, largely in reaction to gradualism, espouse protest action outside the law (and/or predominant custom) to achieve ultimately legitimate ends. The Congress on Racial Equality and the Northern Student Movement, like the Freedom Democratic Party and the Student Nonviolent Coordinating Committee of the South, both advocate sit-ins, marches, and demonstrations, primarily in the South but sometimes in the North, to integrate through peaceful presence illegally segregated facilities. Their methods presuppose, as Louis Lomax has written, "that direct mass action is the only way for Negroes to realize the practical results of the towering legal decisions the N.A.A.C.P. has won."[27]

To the left of them, along the spectrum, would be extremist movements that, in Wilson Record's definition, deviate—in method or goal or both—from the usual pattern. "They seek to withdraw the colored group from society as a whole or to change society in some fundamental way, rather than integrate Negroes into society as it exists."[28] The more radical white-inspired reform groups offered Afro-Americans more promises of immediate equality (if not favored status) than the liberals did, as well as intimations of international connections. The Communist Party U.S.A. tried to dominate extremist sentiment with all sorts of front organizations and bands of informal follow travellers. However, it failed to understand real Afro-American desires (the most famous faux pas being the advocacy of a black republic within America) and instead too often revealed its exploitation of Afro-Americans, regardless of their ambitions, often to ends contrary to their benefits.[29]

Even further to the left would lie black-inspired groups favoring radical, black-nationalist separatism which, following Richard T. Greener (ironically personally fair-skinned) in the late nineteenth century, have "urged Negroes to develop nationalism, to seek for themselves a homeland in Africa, or strive to build a strong, self-sufficient all-Negro community whenever possible."[30] Later separatist groups often promised violent overthrow of the white hegemony in America, sometimes by supernatural means. As Malcolm X, the one-time New York leader of Elijah Muhammad's Nation of Islam and later founder of his own nationalist movement, succinctly expressed it, "The Black Muslims will inherit the earth, particularly America."[31] Vividly important in the short run, these groups attempt to invert the Manichean color symbolism (white equals good; black, bad) that so plagues the Afro-American psyche—supposedly to give lower-class urban blacks more self-pride and race-pride than they had previously been able to acquire.[32]

Historically, this separatist tradition includes Marcus Garvey and his Universal Negro Improvement Association, W. D. Fard, Noble Drew Ali, Elijah Muhammad, Malcolm X, and lesser nationalists; their followings have ranged in size from a handful to about 100,000.[33] Although separatist groups attracted a poorer stratum of Afro-Americans than the white-connected movements, their influence so far has been confined largely to publicity for their ideas and beneficial effects upon the spiritual dignity of their membership, rather than any significant impact upon the politics of Afro-America. As no less sympathetic observer than Myrdal concluded, "A Negro movement in America is doomed to ultimate dissolution and collapse if it cannot gain white support."[34]

Another radical alternative for African-Americans, quite different in goal, is expatriation at their own effort; and the expatriate's choice of a suitable foreign country is often a reflection of his or her politics at home. Many a black Communist traveled to Russia, but even the most sympathetic found it a nicer place to visit than to reside.[35] Some Afro-American Communists who had spurned the opportunity to live in Russia later joined some strains of American black nationalists in regarding Africa as a possible new home. In 1957 Paul Robeson, his passport withheld by the State Department, told *Ebony*'s Carl T. Rowan, "Spiritually I've been a part of Africa for a long time."[36] Late in his life, Du Bois, once granted his passport, renounced his American citizenship and emigrated to Ghana, where he died in 1963. Even later, an embittered South-Carolina-born, New York-matured novelist like Julian Mayfield, who informally aligned himself with non-Muslim black nationalists, settled in Ghana.[37] However, of the few who were able to sample Africa, even fewer stayed; for, as Harold R. Isaacs discovered in numerous interviews, "American Negroes have been rediscovering Africa. In doing so, they are not regaining their identity as long-lost Africans but reshaping their identity as Americans."[38] Some Afro-Americans emigrated to Latin American metropolises, such as Mexico City, which attracted the fathers of both Langston Hughes and Lorraine Hansberry, curiously. Even fewer went to the West Indies, which remains more the "homeland" of the West Indian immigrant (and only sometimes his children) whose culture is quite different from that of native Afro-Americans. The most popular goal of expatriation is the European continent, which has offered Afro-Americans, albeit in small numbers, considerably more social freedom. While those few able to afford it stayed for periods in Europe, "It has been only the writers," according to the historian Richard Bardolph, "plus a sprinkling of artists and entertainers—who have manifested any disposition to remain in Europe."[39] However, writers, especially, often find they suffer an alienation different from that experienced at home—that, as James Baldwin wrote, "They had been divorced from their origins."[40]

Superimposed above the two large categories of alternatives outlined before are three avenues of possible choice that straddle both the North and South. The first, religion, is not political per se, but each religious choice either embodies or implies some kind of political suggestions that are usually communicated to its faithful followers. The potential political power of the black church has always lain in mobilizing its numbers; but historically Afro-American ministers, except those of such avowedly political religions as the Black Muslims, have generally espoused the politics of social resignation. As Gunnar Myrdal wrote in 1944, "They have favored a passive acceptance of one's worldly condition and, indeed, have seen their main function in providing escape and consolation to the sufferers."[41] In more recent years, however, a number of black ministers of orthodox affiliations have initiated and supported political protests in their communities, often fostering and organizing nonviolent demonstrations. In short, then, religion, while not explicitly political, wields such power and respect in the black community that it is inevitably tied to politics.

A second choice is open only to the few who happen, for various reasons, to be born with such fair skin color they can easily pass into white society. According to Saunders Redding, approximately four million people with some Negro ancestry have blended into white society. "Many 'white' people eminent in public life, in industry, in government and the arts," he continues, "are known by Negroes to be Negro."[42] Although "passing," as it is called, is not in the strictest sense a political alternative available to all, it has political overtones, both in the actual sense of breaking the bonds of one's heritage for a new life and, especially to imaginative writers, in its symbolic sense of

Afro-American total assimilation into white society as it presently exists. Intermarriage, also, carries symbolic suggestions similar to and yet different from passing. Neither alternative is wholly without precedent.

The third of those alternatives likewise proposed in both North and South was historically even more rare—the creation of an independent African-American community within the United States. Perhaps the first actual settlement was Nashoba in Western Tennessee in the late 1820s, but it failed from an absence of competent leadership. The largest and most famous Afro-American entity, albeit brief in duration, was the Port Royal community in South Carolina's Sea Islands soon after the Civil War.[43] Variations on the scheme include Isaiah T. Montgomery's wholly Afro-American communities in the late nineteenth century, first in Davis Bend and then in Mound Bayou, Mississippi, both of them run literally as private fiefs; and although the latter settlement survived its founder's death, it was always at the mercy of the surrounding Mississippi whites. According to Saunders Redding, "[Montgomery's] daughter was killed like a common criminal by a white sheriff." As Myrdal wrote of Mound Bayou in the early 1940s, "While Negroes vote unhampered in the local elections, . . . their votes are not always accepted in country, state and federal elections."[44] In spite of its modest success, Mound Bayou inspired few imitations. In more recent times, the ideal of separatism has been more publicized than realized, and the scope of the dream from time to time expands from a community or two to a belt of states. Minister Malcolm X, when still an officer in Elijah Muhammad's movement, begged of a white audience, "Just give us a portion of this country that we can call our own."[45] Although the notion of separate communities has always had a currency of fluctuating value, it has never had much practical support from Afro-Americans.

As far as the strategy of this book is concerned, whether or not these four novelists had these particular solutions clearly in mind or viewed political alternatives in different categories is beside the point; likewise irrelevant are the questions of whether or not they planned their novels as tests or illustrations of political ideas or whether or not they regarded their new novels as commentaries upon previous novels (though often they seem to be). "Never trust the artist, trust the tale. The proper function of the critic is to save the tale from the artist who created it," D. H. Lawrence once remarked.[46] Following this prescription, the following chapters analyze closely and elaborately *what the novels say* about Afro-American politics and assume that what is found is fairly close to what the authors intended.

What finally emerges from all these novels is a scathing and thorough critique not only of American life itself but also of the standard political solutions for bettering Afro-American life. In all the novels, in sum, panaceas are tested and all are found wanting. Thus, in the last novels of both Du Bois and Wright, the protagonist emigrates from America completely disgusted by racist enemies, disillusioned with the race's "friends," somewhat ashamed of his own people. However, neither novelist was able to portray with any adequate fullness the life of his characters abroad, perhaps because they could be only ashamed of the Mandarin existence of an Afro-American intellectual in Europe or Africa.[47] In his one novel, Ellison too posits a kind of emigration to an underground cave—an escape more credible as a symbol for all emigrations or willful isolation than as an actual event—only to show that this solution too is inadequate. In this respect, the tentative and qualified affirmation at the end of Ellison's novel has its parallel in post–World War II Afro-American intellectual thought and, indeed, in Afro-American life itself.

NOTES

1. Saunders Redding, "The Negro Writer and His Relationship to His Roots," in Abraham Chapman, ed., *Black Voices* (New York, 1968), 612.

2. Robin G. Collingwood, *The Idea of History* (New York, 1956), 245–46. See also Emery Neff, *The Poetry of History* (New York, 1947),

and Stanley Edgar Hyman, *The Tangled Bank* (New York, 1962).

3. Isaiah Berlin, *The Hedgehog and the Fox* (New York, 1957), 30.

4. For an interpretation of history in Thomas Pynchon's first novel, see Irving Feldman, "Keeping Cool," *Commentary*, *36* (September 1963), 258–60.

5. Finis Farr, *Black Champion* (London, 1964).

6. Harvey Breit, "Frank Yerby," *The Writer Observed* (New York, 1961), 127–29; Arna Bontemps, "Reflections on Richard Wright," in Herbert Hill, ed., *Anger, and Beyond* (New York, 1966), 203.

7. Robert A. Bone, *The Negro Novel in America* (New Haven, 1958), 43, 45–46, 96, 152.

8. Georg Lukacs, *The Historical Novel* (Boston, 1963), 19, *passim.*

9. Stanley Edgar Hyman, *The Promised End* (New York, 1963), 120.

10. Albert L. Murray, "Something Different, Something More," in Herbert Hill, ed., *Anger, and Beyond*, 129; Ralph Ellison, *Shadow and Act* (New York, 1964), 78; Ellison, *Going to the Territory* (New York, 1986).

11. August Meier, *Negro Thought in America, 1880–1915* (Ann Arbor, 1963), *passim.*

12. Gunnar Myrdal, *An American Dilemma* (New York, 1964), 769, 786.

13. Ralph Ellison, *Invisible Man* (New York, 1960), 19–20.

14. Stanley Edgar Hyman, *The Promised End*, 297. See also Bernard Wolfe, "Uncle Remus and the Malevolent Rabbit," *Commentary*, *3* (July 1949), and Bernard Wolfe, "Ecstatic in Blackface," in Chandler Brossard, ed., *The Scene Before You* (New York, 1955).

15. John Hope Franklin, *Reconstruction After the Civil War* (Chicago, 1962), 85–103.

16. Rayford W. Logan, *The Betrayal of the Negro* (New York, 1965); C. Vann Woodward, *The Strange Career of Jim Crow* (New York, 1966); and Paul E. Buck, *The Road to Reunion* (New York, 1959), 294–307.

17. Arnold Rose, "Postscript: Twenty Years Later," in Myrdal, *An American Dilemma*, xxx-xxxi. See also Martin Luther King, Jr., *Stride Toward Freedom* (New York, 1958) and Howard Zinn, *SNCC: The New Abolitionists* (Boston, 1964), 11, 23, 41, *passim.*

18. Herbert Aptheker, *American Negro Slave Revolts* (New York, 1943), 163, *passim*. See also Aptheker, ed., *A Documentary History of the Negro People in the United States* (New York, 1962, 1964).

19. Julian Mayfield, "Challenge to Negro Leadership," *Commentary*, *31* (April 1961), 297–305.

20. Stanley Elkins, *Slavery* (New York, 1963), 136–37.

21. Walter L. Fleming, " 'Pap' Singleton, the Moses of the Colored Exodus," *American Journal of Sociology*, *15* (July 1909).

22. See Ralph Ellison, *Shadow and Act*, xiii–xiv; Robert A. Bone, "Ralph Ellison and the Uses of Imagination," in Hill, ed., *Anger, and Beyond*, 87. On the Afro-American culture of the Southwest, see Marshall Stearns, *The Story of Jazz* (New York, 1958), 151; Bill Simon, "Charlie Christian," in Nat Shapiro and Nat Hentoff, eds., *The Jazz Makers* (New York, 1957); Franklin S. Drigges, "Kansas City and the Southwest," in Nat Hentoff and Albert McCarthy, eds., *Jazz* (New York, 1961).

23. Meier, *Negro Thought in America*, 66; Richard B. Moore, "Africa Conscious Harlem," in John Hendrik Clarke, ed., *Harlem, U.S.A.* (Berlin, 1964), 58–61. See also Miles Mark Fisher, *Negro Slave Songs in the United States* (New York, 1963).

24. Arna Bontemps and Jack Conroy, *They Seek a City* (Garden City, 1945), *passim*.

25. Louis Lomax, *When the Word is Given . . .* (Cleveland, 1963), 77. See also St. Clair Drake and Horace R. Cayton, *Black Metropolis* (New York, 1962), *passim*.

26. Louis Lomax, *The Negro Revolt* (New York, 1963), 224–35, 118; Myrdal, *An American Dilemma*, 819ff; James Q. Wilson, "The Negro in Politics," in Stephen R. Graubard, ed., *The Negro American* (Cambridge, 1965).

27. Lomax, *The Negro Revolt*, 158.

28. Wilson Record, "Extremist Movements Among American Negroes," *Phylon*, *17*, 1 (1956), 18.

29. See Irving Howe and Lewis Coser, *The American Communist Party* (Boston, 1957), 204–16; Wilson Record, *The Negro and the Communist Party* (Chapel Hill, N.C., 1951).

30. E. U. Essien-Udom, *Black Nationalism* (New York, 1964), 328.

31. Quoted by Lomax, *When the Word*, 92. See also C. Eric Lincoln, *The Black Muslims in America* (Boston, 1961).

32. Essien-Udom, *Black Nationalism*, 361–65.

33. For estimates of membership in Garvey's group, see Edmund David Cronon, *Black Moses* (Madison, Wis., 1955), 204–7.

34. Myrdal, *An American Dilemma*, 749.

35. Langston Hughes, "Moscow Movie," in Herbert Hill, ed., *Soon One Morning* (New York, 1963), 124. See also Homer Smith, *Black Man in Red Russia* (Chicago, 1964).

36. Carl T. Rowan, "Has Paul Robeson Betrayed the Negro?" *Ebony*, *12* (October 1957), 31–42. See also Paul Robeson, *Here I Stand* (London, 1958), 95.

37. Julian Mayfield, et al., "The Young Radicals: A Symposium," *Dissent*, *9* (Spring 1962), 144.

38. Harold R. Isaacs, "Integration and the Negro Mood," *Commentary*, *34* (December 1962), 487.

39. Richard Bardolph, *The Negro Vanguard* (New York, 1961), 380. See also William Gardner Smith, "Black Man in Europe," *Holiday*, *37* (January 1965).

40. James Baldwin, *Nobody Knows My Name* (New York, 1961), 4.

41. Myrdal, *An American Dilemma*, 873. See also Elmer T. Clark, *The Small Sects in America* (New York, 1949), 116–30.

42. Saunders Redding, *On Being Negro in America* (New York, 1962), 116. See also Lerone Bennett, Jr., *Before the Mayflower* (Chicago, 1962), 267–69; Drake and Cayton, *Black Metropolis*, 159–71; and Walter White, "Why I Remain a Negro," *Saturday Review Reader* (New York, 1951), 3.

43. See William H. Pease and Jane H. Pease, *Black Utopia* (Madison, Wis., 1963); Elmer T. Clark, *The Small Sects in America* (New York, 1949), 151–53; Willie Lee Rose, *Rehearsal for Reconstruction* (Indianapolis, Ind., 1964).

44. Saunders Redding, *The Lonesome Road* (Garden City, N.Y.: 1958), 125; Myrdal, *An American Dilemma*, 480n.

45. Malcolm X, quoted in Lomax, *When the Word*, 130.

46. D. H. Lawrence, *Studies in Classic American Literature* (New York, 1964), 2.

47. The novelist William Demby portrays this subject in *The Catacombs* (New York, 1965).

two

James Weldon Johnson

James Weldon Johnson was an avant-gardist, who fathered modern Afro-American fiction. Within *The Autobiography of an Ex-Colored Man*, Johnson established the concept of the invisible man. It was on that rock that Wright and Ellison built their church.

—Joe Johnson, in a personal letter
to Richard Kostelanetz (1990)

James Weldon Johnson's sole novel, *The Autobiography of an Ex-Colored Man* (1912), treats a subject recurrent in early African-American writing, the experience of a very fair-skinned African-American who passes into white society. Indeed, the theme appeared in what was long regarded as the first novel attributed to a black American author, *Clotel, or the President's Daughter* (1853), by William Wells Brown, an expatriate abolitionist. In the original edition, his mulatto protagonist Clotel is traced to Thomas Jefferson's lecherous adventures; however, in the later American edition, as Robert A. Bone observed, "An anonymous senator is substituted for Jefferson, and the plot is altered accordingly."[1] The point of Wells Brown's novel is that once Clotel's part-black origins are disclosed, she is still considered a slave and, thus, subject to recapture. Charles Chesnutt, perhaps the first major

Afro-American fiction writer, portrayed in *The House Behind the Cedars* (1900) a young woman, Rena, the master's daughter by a colored mistress, who decides to pass into white society. Upon the eve of her wedding to a white man, her racial background is revealed, and as a result the marriage is cancelled. Heartbroken, she lets her life disintegrate. The moral of Chesnutt's story holds that the major risk of passing is that discovery can ruin one's life. Given this background, it is scarcely surprising that a spate of novels about passing appeared in the 1920s: Jessie Fauset's *There Is Confusion* (1924) and *Plum Bun* (1928), Nella Larsen's *Quicksand* (1928), and Walter White's *Flight* (1926).[2]

James Weldon Johnson's novel is an unsentimental and more complex exploration of the subject and a superior work of art, although esthetically marred by numerous polemical digressions, sometimes of considerable perception, on "the Negro problem." Originally published anonymously by Sherman, French and Company in 1912, *The Autobiography of an Ex-Colored Man* was restored to its author when it was republished fifteen years later, at the height of the negro renaissance, with Carl Van Vechten's introduction. The book is a fictional memoir whose first-person narrator is so intimate and honest with his readers that they would, unless warned otherwise, accept his words as authentic autobiography; a later, equally successful model of autobiographical artifice is Ralph Ellison's *Invisible Man*. In fact, *The Autobiography*, like Ellison's novel, is not in the least autobiographical, except in the sense that certain events have their symbolic equivalents in Johnson's own life.[3] The effectiveness of the artifice is, of course, a basic measure of Johnson's fictional artistry.

The novel's theme is the many ambiguities of passing—moral, political, emotional; and its predominant action is the nameless narrator's shifting sympathies for white or black identity. Born in Georgia, the son of a white man by his family's favorite black servant, the narrator grows up with his mother in Connecticut, attending a racially mixed elementary school. He unwittingly identifies with white peers in the squabbles with "the niggers" until a white teacher says to his class, "I wish all of the white scholars to stand for a moment":

> I rose with the others. The teacher looked at me and, calling my name, said: "You sit down for the present, and rise with the others." I did not quite understand her, and questioned "Ma'm?" She repeated, with a softer tone in her voice: "You sit down now, and rise with the others." (16)

However, as his community is not aggressively racist, the narrator remains only dimly aware of his racial origins until high school. There, a dark-skinned friend nicknamed "Shiny" instills in the narrator some awareness of his heritage:

> I read with studious interest everything I could find relating to coloured men who had gained prominence. My heroes had been King David, then Robert the Bruce; now Frederick Douglass was enshrined in the place of honor. (46)

Thus, when forced to select a college from the two possible alternatives presented to him—his father's recommendation, Harvard; or his mother's, Atlanta—he decides on the latter. Once there, however, he finds himself unable to register because his "inheritance" (money from his father) is stolen. He thinks of explaining his predicament to the school's authorities; but as he approaches their offices, "I paused, undecided for a moment; then turned and slowly retraced my steps, and so changed the whole course of my life." (63) In traveling to Florida, he undergoes a symbolic dark night of suffering in a womblike setting. "Twelve hours doubled up in a porter's basket for soiled linen, not being able to straighten up. The air was hot and suffocating and the smell of damp towels and used linen was sickening." (65) He emerges reborn to a new existence in the African-American community of Jacksonville.

As a cigar-maker, he learns of both the impregnable structure of Southern discrimination and the exclusive habits of the black middle class. Finding himself doomed to remain an outsider in the South, unfulfilled in his ambitions, this narrator, like so many analogous characters in later African-American fiction, heads north to New York City. Once there, he gravitates to the major black bohemia of the early twentieth century, in the West Twenties between Sixth and Seventh Avenues, first making his way as a successful gambler and then as a pianist of ragtime music. In this milieu he discovers freedom of movement but little discernible stability—opportunistic drifters, white widows on the make, sporting men capable of sudden violence. A disagreeable experience with the last element drives the narrator to befriend a millionaire white man who, out of admiration for his piano playing, offers to become his patron. At the novel's turning point, the narrator and his benefactor go off to Europe; and the narrator, now posing as a white man, enters high-class international society.

Still, he does not claim his white identity at once. At a Paris theater, he recognizes the man two seats away as his father, but he refuses the temptation to announce his presence. Later becoming disillusioned with his patron's way of life—a constant quest for novelty to assuage the boredom of purposelessness— the narrator remembers his childhood ambition to become an Afro-American composer and collector of African-American folk materials. Despite the millionaire's not-unperceptive warning that "the idea you have of making a Negro out of yourself is nothing more than a sentiment," the narrator returns to America to pursue his self-determined task. In each Southern town he visits he is faced with the possibility of passing for white, but each time he reaffirms blackness:

> In thus traveling about through the country I was sometimes amused on arriving at some little railroad station town to be taken for and treated as a white man, and six hours later, when it was learned that I was stopping at the house of the colored preacher or school-teacher, to note the attitude of the whole town change. (172)

Just as an earlier incident of violence propelled him out of black
bohemia into his white patron's beneficence, so his witnessing of
a Southern lynching initiates another collapse of personal purpose
and integrity. The narrator experiences a second rebirth with a
new vow: "I would neither disclaim the black race nor claim the
white race; but . . . I would change my name, raise a mustache,
and let the world take me for what it would." (190) Behind
this decision is a patent rationalization for cowardice and pure
self-interest: "Shame at being identified with a people that would
with impunity be treated worse than animals." (191) However, it
is still a credible outcome of his experience.

He returns to New York, takes a well-paying job, invests his
money in real estate, and strikes up a relationship with a Caucasian
woman. The specter of his past identity confronts him when he
and his fiancee accidentally meet his childhood friend Shiny in
a museum; but in cutting short Shiny's approach, the narrator
rejects a last tie to the past.[4] He marries the white woman, who
bears him a boy and a girl, only to die suddenly; and he assumes
responsibility for his children. The book's final passage conveys
his continued ambivalence over passing:

> My love for children makes me glad that I am what I am
> and keeps me from desiring to be otherwise; and yet, when
> I sometimes open a little box in which I still keep my fast
> yellowing [music] manuscripts, the only tangible remnants
> of a vanished dream, a dead ambition, a sacrificed talent,
> I cannot repress the thought that, after all, I have chosen
> the lesser part, that I have sold my birthright for a mess of
> pottage. (211)

The price of passing is not only a loss of heritage and the sacrifice of one's self-chosen mission but guilt over an opportunistic
materialism equal to that of Esau in Genesis (25:29–34). So
famished from toiling in the fields, we remember, Esau frivolously
exchanged "his birthright" with his brother Jacob for "bread and
pottage of lentils."

Some of the book's meaning stems from its relationship to Afro-American folk blues, that tightly organized lyric form in which the singer narrates the reason for his sadness, usually attributed to his failure to attain the ideal role he conceives for himself. In a successful blues song, the singer makes his personal predicament a realized metaphor for the human condition.[5] Here the subject of the blues is selling out one's dreams for material rewards. Johnson was, of course, aware of the folk blues tradition, not only from his experience writing show tunes with his brother Rosamund but also from a desire to appropriate the heritage for literature. In his actual autobiography, *Along the Way* (1933), Johnson wrote of his early days:

> I now began to grope toward a realization of the importance of the American Negro's cultural background and his creative folk-art, and to speculate on the superstructure of conscious art that might be reared upon this.[6]

This statement echoes what Johnson wrote in the introduction to *The Book of American Negro Poetry* (1922):

> What the colored poet in the United States needs to do is something like Synge did for the Irish; he needs to find a form that will express the racial spirit by symbols from within rather than by symbols from without, such as the mere mutilation of English spelling and punctuation.[7]

In the novel, then, Johnson's narrator expresses a disenchantment of a special kind—a blues about being white, but black. Passing produces not only the individual's alienation from his natural milieu but feelings of the blues, expressed particularly as a guilty self-identification with Abraham's least-favored grandson, Esau. In the political sense then, the novel suggests that passing—an African-American's total assimilation into white culture—signifies opportunistic rejection of one's heritage for the meagre "mess of pottage" of material comfort.

NOTES

1. Robert A. Bone, *The Negro Novel in America* (New Haven, Conn., 1958), 30. Regarding William Wells Brown, see Richard Bardolph, *The Negro Vanguard* (New York, 1961), 66–70.

2. See Hugh M. Gloster, *Negro Voices in American Fiction* (Chapel Hill, N.C., 1948).

3. Though quite dark in complexion, Johnson could pass for a Latin American by speaking Spanish; he once accompanied a Spanish-speaking white friend in the first-class coach on a Southern train. John Hope Franklin, "Introduction," *Three Negro Classics* (New York, 1965), xv; James Weldon Johnson, *Along the Way* (New York, 1933), 65.

4. According to folklorist Roger D. Abrahams, the name "Shiny" is "generic for any male Negro." *Deep Down in the Jungle . . .* (Hatboro, Pa., 1964), 116.

5. For insights into the esthetic character and purpose of the blues, this writer is indebted to an unpublished paper by Stanley Edgar Hyman that subsequently appeared in his posthumous book, *The Critic's Credentials* (New York, 1978). For an abridged version of Hyman's ideas, see "Those Trans-Atlantic Blues," *The New Leader*, 44, 35 (October 16, 1961), 24–25. See also Harold Courlander, *Negro Folk Music, U.S.A.* (New York, 1963), 128–45; Ralph Ellison, *Shadow and Act* (New York, 1964), 78–79.

6. Johnson, *Along the Way*, 133.

7. Johnson, ed., *The Book of American Negro Poetry* (New York, 1922), 41.

three

W.E.B. Du Bois

To whom does Richard Wright address himself? Certainly not to the universal man. The essential characteristic of the notion of the universal man is that he is not involved in any particular age, and that he is no more and no less moved by the lot of the Negroes of Louisiana than by that of the Roman slaves in the time of Spartacus. The universal man can think of nothing but universal values. He is a pure and abstract affirmation of the inalienable right of man. But neither can Wright think of intending his books for the white racists of Virginia or South Carolina whose minds are made up in advance and who will not open them. Nor to the black peasants of the bayous who can not read. . . . He is addressing himself to the cultivated Negroes of the North and the white Americans of good-will (intellectuals, democrats of the left, radicals, CIO workers).
                    –Jean-Paul Sartre, "Why Write?" (1949)

I

William Edward Burghardt Du Bois had established himself as a thoroughly professional writer long before he published, at the age of forty-three, his first novel, *The Quest of the Silver Fleece* (1911). As an ambitious and self-confident teenager, he became the western Massachusetts correspondent for the New

York *Globe*, an Afro-American newspaper; as an undergraduate at Fisk, an Afro-American college in Tennessee, he edited the college newspaper; as a graduate student at Harvard, he prepared a lecture on how, in Elliott M. Rudwick's summary, "The race [in America] had made no contributions to civilization and was existing on a primitive level."[1] He completed his Ph.D. thesis on "The Suppression of the African Slave Trade" in 1895, becoming the first Afro-American to earn a doctorate at Harvard; and this thesis appeared in book form a year later. Soon after, he embarked on a prolific writing career that included both scholarly works like *The Philadelphia Negro: A Social Study* (1899) and numerous, more popular articles in national magazines and newspapers. Some of his early essays were collected in that much-reprinted classic, *The Souls of Black Folk* (1903). As a writer, Du Bois had mastered a variety of expository forms from academic essay to polemic to poetic prose-pieces (as in the famous essay on the death of his son, included in *Black Folk*). Indeed, writing became such an instinctive response to the events in his life that even such an anxious experience as hurrying back to Atlanta to help quell the race riots of 1906 inspired him to write, while on the train, his single most poetic piece of prose, "A Litany at Atlanta," which James Weldon Johnson later anthologized as "poetry."[2]

However, Du Bois's sensibility, honed on those expository forms that require an unsentimental tone and intellectual coherence, was slow to adjust to the necessities of fiction, for his first novel suggests that Du Bois may have looked upon the writing of fiction as an opportunity to relax his intellectual muscles. *The Quest of the Silver Fleece* is striking, first of all, for the richness and variousness of its political concerns—an attribute of all of Du Bois's fiction; yet the novel's major failure stems from Du Bois's inability to weave all the strands of a multiple plot into a coherent whole. Its overarching action—introduced at its start, mentioned intermittently, and concluded at its end—is an off-and-on romance between Blessed Alwyn, sometimes the novel's apparent protagonist, and Zora, a romantic figure with no surname other than "child of the swamp." (44) Another thread of the plot portrays the efforts of a nondescript white woman, indicatively named "Miss Smith," to run a school for blacks in Alabama. A third deals with the Cresswell family, white Southern landlords, in their attempt, first, to force down the price of cotton and then corner the market and, second, to expand their landholdings. A fourth strand follows two white Northerners, Mary and John Taylor, sister and brother, through their adventures in the South—the sister to teach at the school, only to become disillusioned and, then, for lack of other available suitors, to marry into the Cresswell family; the brother to make a lucrative business deal with the white landlords who, in turn, exploit Afro-American labor. John Taylor's major mission, as Du Bois writes, was "to apply his knowledge of the world's nakedness [its need for cotton] and the black man's toil in such a way as to bring himself wealth." (55) A fifth plot is the possibility of Afro-American advance through orthodox politics. Yet another development, introduced late in the novel, follows the efforts of the underdogs, black and sometimes white, to disrupt the machinery of exploitation.

All strands except the first—the romance—incorporate political significances. Smith is a benevolent white Southerner, immensely devoted to raising the educational level of the Afro-American community and making it more self-sufficient. Despite the local whites' condescending attitude toward her and her work, she endeavors to send her best students to the black universities. Apprehensive about her purposes, the local landholders harass and vilify her. At one point, recognizing that she needs money, they give her a mortgage on her school property in hopes that, when she fails payments, they can foreclose. At another point they attempt to persuade a prospective big donor to stipulate that the school's operation be subject to a board of local white trustees.

The third thread deals with the character of the Southern economy. The Cresswells recognize that if American cotton is to compete successfully on the world labor market, it must be produced by the cheapest labor possible. As Colonel Cresswell puts it, "American cotton-spinning supremacy is built upon cheap cotton, cheap cotton is built on cheap niggers." (160) The education of Afro-Americans for anything more ambitious than manual labor is to be feared, while excessive charity toward them and the intrusions of outside agitators are to be discouraged, all for the same reason—disruption of the current exploitation of labor. Moreover, the cotton lords believed that their laborers should be encouraged to go into debt with their regular employers in order to discourage their migration elsewhere. The novel's plot, in its fourth line, also discusses white Northerners in the South; and the portraits suggest that even if they came South with good intentions, they can only exploit Afro-Americans for ulterior ends—Mary Taylor to find a husband; John Taylor to make money. This is another way of saying that, as much as Northern whites may sympathize with the African-American plight, they offer, aside from charity, little direct aid.

The fifth strand, which probably receives more thorough treatment in the novel than the others, illustrates in no uncertain terms that Afro-Americans in legitimate politics are either dupes, as Blessed Alwyn was in his younger days, or self-seeking opportunists. The scenes in Washington, D.C., clarify that white politicians of both parties look upon Afro-American leaders as magnets to swing blocks of Afro-American votes. In return white politicians extend patronage only to black leaders who split the spoils with their immediate benefactors. Neither white nor black politicians, the novel suggests, do anything to aid the mass of black people. The novel also intimates that the white leaders and/or their agents directly bribe the editors of Afro-American newspapers to influence the black vote.

Although Du Bois's picture of the Afro-American plight would seem to demand some decisive conclusions about possibilities for political change, the novel is actually vague and, in the end, somewhat contradictory. The novel conveys what Elliott M. Rudwick has identified as Du Bois's major characteristic ambivalence—on one hand he believed that Afro-Americans should band together to better their lot through a segregated culture; on the other, he argued that his people should collaborate with sympathetic whites to overthrow racial barriers.[3] Exemplifying the latter theme, an unnamed white character murmurs in the courtroom, apparently with Du Bois's approval, " 'Durned if I don't think these white slaves and black slaves had ought ter git together.' " (395) Yet, Du Bois also has his nominal hero, Bles Alwyn—clearly an example of what Du Bois elsewhere called "the talented tenth" of his race[4]—speak of a totally Afro-American cooperative within the South, where all the shareholders would till the common land and share equally in the profits:

> We want to centre here agencies to make life better. We want all sorts of industries; we want a little hospital with a resident physician and two or three nurses; we want a cooperative store for buying supplies; we want a cotton gin and saw mill; and in the future other things. (404)

The point is that if the Afro-American community can produce better cotton than the whites, as Bles and Zora did as teenagers in their small plot of land, then an Afro-American combine could successfully compete in the existing free market. In the end, the novel would seem tentatively to echo the historic Mound Bayou experiment by favoring cooperative separatism within Southern capitalism.

In comparison with his first novel, Du Bois's second work of fiction, *Dark Princess* (1928), has two literary virtues—a more effective structure and greater political coherence. As a novel, it is otherwise distinctly inferior to its predecessor—less grounded in worldly realities (its subtitle, *A Romance*, is perhaps intended to signify an apology), more sentimental and exaggerated in its characterizations, less credible in the progress of its events, and more melodramatic in its transitions. The plot is a favorite for Afro-American fiction—the adventures of a talented and rather idealistic young man; and the novel reflects the less exclusive form of black nationalism—a kind of catholic colored internationalism—that had preoccupied Du Bois for many years

before. In 1919, we remember, he had organized the first of four
Pan-African Conferences, the last of which met in 1927, the year
before *Dark Princess* appeared.[5]

The novel opens with a scene at the University of Manhattan's
"great medical center" at 165th Street. The new dean, a white
Southerner by background, tells Matthew Towns, a black honor
student, that he is forbidden to register for the course in obstetrics.
"Do you think white women patients are going to have a nigger
doctor delivering their babies?" (4) Realizing that white American
society, even in its higher echelons, will not admit him as an equal,
Towns leaves the United States for Berlin. There he encounters
the Indian Princess Kautilya, who in turn introduces him into
her circle of colored intellectuals—Chinese, Egyptian, Indian,
Japanese, and Arab. Though Towns finds them more stimulating
than people back home, he still feels the need to return to
America. Nonetheless, the Princess's friendship, as well as what
she represents, confronts him again in the novel.

Back in New York, Towns meets Perigua, a black nationalist
who somewhat resembles the historic Marcus Garvey, particularly
in his hyperbolic speaking style; but whereas Garvey preached
expatriation and black separatism within America, Perigua stands
for reverse violence within the South: "There's a lynching belt,"
he says. "We'll blow it to hell with dynamite from airplanes.
And then when the Ku Klux Klan meets sometime, we'll blow
them up. Terrorism, revenge is our program." (46)

To avenge the lynching, Perigua plans to sabotage a special
train carrying Ku Klux Klan leaders to a Chicago meeting.
However, Towns, traveling on the train as a porter and an
accomplice to the plot, discovers that the Princess Kautilya and
her entourage are also passengers. He stops the train in the nick
of time, and the bomb damages nothing more than track. The
incident confirms an Afro-American minister's earlier warning
about reverse violence as a political strategy: "What good?
Murder, and murder mainly of the innocent." (165) Moreover,
Perigua, like the historic Garvey, appears to have more charis-
matic appeal than capacities to organize a following, and the

novel suggests that this personal deficiency would limit the effectiveness of his movement. Just before he halts the train, Towns decides a better strategy would be gradual reform, "the slow, sure gathering growth of power and vision, expanding and uniting with the thought of a wider, better world." (91)

Because of his complicity in the attempted train wreck, Matthew Towns is imprisoned and then, thanks to the Honorable Sammy Scott, "a leading colored politician of Chicago," released before his term expires. Scott, aware of the power of publicity, campaigns for Towns's release; as the young man had fortuitously acquired the image of a race martyr, Scott's efforts on his behalf will gain a favorable response from black voters. Scott himself represents a twofold nexus—"between white political leadership and the voters of the black community" and between political-legal power and commercially organized crime.

> Sammy began business in 1910 by selling the right to gamble, keep houses of prostitution, and commit petty theft, to certain men, white and black, who paid him in cash. With this cash he bribed the city officials and police to let these people alone and he paid a little army of henchmen to organize the Negro voters and see that they voted for officials that could be bribed. (110)

His operating assumption is that if an African-American is to rise in municipal politics, he must deliver black votes to the white candidates who court (and pay for) his favor and, incidentally, also control the relations between shady enterprise and law enforcement agencies. Morally weakened by his stay in prison, Towns joins Scott's political machine and becomes, in Scott's eyes, "an invaluable lieutenant," eventually marrying Sara Andrews, Scott's secretary. A woman of boundless ambition, Sara pushes Towns to run for Congress; and when enemy politicians threaten to expose a misinterpreted event in Towns's past, she takes charge of his campaign. Although he wins the Congressional seat, Towns slowly drifts away from his wife and begins to feel guilty about

the moral costs of election victory, such as the deceits of his
political platform.

> He was paying a price for power and money. A great, a
> terrible price. He was lying, cheating, stealing. He was fooling
> those poor driven slaves of industry. He had listened to their
> arguments all this afternoon. He had meant now to meet the
> delegation brusquely and tell them railingly that they were
> idiots, that he could do little. (207)

Just before the party honoring his forthcoming trip to Washington, Towns inadvertently encounters the princess at a gathering. Later that evening he publicly announces: "I will not have
your nomination. I'd rather go to hell than to Congress. I'm
through with liars, thieves and hypocrites. The cause that was
dead is alive again. The love that I lost is found." Recognizing
that as a mainline politician he was exploiting his power over his
race primarily for self-advancement, Towns rejects success in the
white American world to reaffirm the colored internationalism he
found as a youth in Berlin, vowing, instead, to exploit himself
to advance his race. He discovers that Kautilya, like himself,
had the opportunity to succeed in the white world, as the wife
of a prominent white Englishman; but she refused his marriage
proposal. Together they realize that all the colored peoples of the
world must unite to take over the land that is rightfully theirs.
Kautilya adds that the dominance of the darker peoples extends
into America:

> Here in Virginia you are at the edge of a black world. The
> black belt of the Congo, the Nile, and the Ganges reaches by
> way of Guinea, Haiti, and Jamaica, like a red arrow, up into
> the heart of white America. Thus I see a mighty synthesis;
> you can work in Africa and Asia right here in America if you
> work in the black belt. (285)

Later she predicts that the revolution of colored people will
succeed. "In 1952, the Dark World goes free—whether in peace

and fostering Friendship with all men, or in Blood and Storm—it is for them—the Pale Masters of Today—to say." (297) From this prediction of the millennium, the novel shifts to Matthew Towns's own salvation, first as the princess's husband and, second, as the acknowledged father of the future Maharajah of Bwodpur. He lives happily ever after, the novel would suggest, in India—a kind of favored expatriation that has been scarcely available to all Afro-Americans.

Du Bois believed at the time in this sort of possible millennium, largely because, one suspects, he remained impervious to the realities of color prejudice around the world. With a bluntness that does not betray a sharp perception, Professor Edward M. East criticized Du Bois's position as the fantasy of an innocent. "The Japanese and the Chinese," East wrote, "despise each other, and both feel superior to the brown and the black, and the Hindu has more caste tabus than either."[6] Indeed, Du Bois himself soon discarded this dream and, in 1933, reverted to a design for Afro-American self-segregation within the United States. He also ceased publishing fiction for nearly three decades, perhaps because his novels had few admirers, even among critics similar in race. In one of their subprefaces to *The Negro Caravan* (1941), Sterling Brown, Arthur P. Davis, and Ulysses Lee, English professors all, declare Du Bois "inferior to [Charles P.] Chesnett as a novelist."[7]

Some twenty-nine years after *Dark Princess*, in 1957, in his own eighty-ninth year, Du Bois published *The Ordeal of Mansart*, the first volume of a historical trilogy he entitled *Black Flame*. In 1959 the second volume appeared, *Mansart Builds a School*, and in 1961 the third, *Worlds of Color*. How much of this trilogy is Du Bois's own work is, for many reasons, a matter worthy of conjecture. It is, after all, rather unusual for an author, even one as energetic and indomitable as Du Bois, to be so productive in his late eighties and early nineties, especially since during this period he also wrote articles, took a trip around the world, received honors from Communist universities and leaders between Prague and Peking (including a Lenin International Peace Prize), made plans to emigrate to Africa where he would edit an encyclopedia, and drafted an autobiography whose manuscript he showed to an interviewer in 1960 and which eventually appeared in 1968.[8] His second wife, Shirley Graham, herself a popular biographer of some note, had started to help Du Bois with his writing as early as 1951, the year after their marriage; for many chapters of Du Bois's 1952 book, *In Battle for Peace*, an outraged memoir of his defense against the U.S. government's charge of subversion, have Graham's postscripts, which, in a similar style, elaborate on points Du Bois made earlier. The style of these late polemics and novels is also conspicuously different from that of his earlier books (though not, however, different from that of his popular journalism for, say, *Crisis*) in that the sentences have become shorter, curter, and simpler. The tone is less condescending, and the representational style of the fiction more realistic. Moreover, Graham has been notoriously protective of her husband, keeping his papers from scholarly researchers, even those who, like Francis Broderick, were previously granted permission to see them. On the other hand, the fictional trilogy does exhibit many of Du Bois's typical critiques and some characteristic ambivalences, as well as his extraordinary knowledge of historical facts and anecdotes. In all, then, it would not be too farfetched to suspect some collaboration between the two writers, but the themes of the novels should be seen as expressions of Du Bois's own thoughts.

Black Flame is a stylistically old-fashioned saga-novel portraying the Mansart family's journey through America. Tom Mansart, born into slavery, fathered Manuel Mansart who had three sons and a daughter, who all, in turn, provided him with several grandchildren; and all of the Mansart family become the novel's protagonist, experiencing many of the political alternatives open to Afro-Americans. The trilogy as a whole, then, becomes a testing—an evaluation and judgment—of these possibilities.

As historical fiction, the trilogy is a remarkable performance, though neglected by all critics except those predisposed to Du Bois's avowed politics. For its breadth and richness of precisely detailed history, *Black Flame* is quite unlike anything else in recent American literature. Esthetically it is in some ways superior to previous Du Bois fiction, being generally less sentimental and romantic in its characterizations, more credible in its plot, and more accurate in its observations of social reality; and for these reasons, as well as its historical comprehensiveness, the trilogy achieves a polemical effectiveness absent from Du Bois's earlier fiction.

The Mansart family progresses through both authentic and imaginary historical events, often including as well as observing identifiable historical characters, some of them still living when the trilogy was first published, such as Herbert Hoover and Du Bois himself. The author modestly identifies himself as "Professor Burghardt" and, functioning as a historical novelist, Du Bois is not at all adverse to quoting his own editorials in the N.A.A.C.P. magazine *Crisis* and then even gauging their impact upon readers like the Mansarts. Immodesty notwithstanding, Du Bois does not exaggerate his own historical importance, for the influence of his writings upon all Afro-Americans, especially the intelligentsia, has been acknowledged by many disinterested observers.[9]

Although *Black Flame* has the veneer of genuine history, Du Bois admits in his postscript to the opening volume to his use of imaginative license, for example, in quoting the thoughts of historical figures. He justifies his method with the following rationale:

The basis of this book is documented and verifiable fact, but the book is not history. On the contrary, I have used fiction to interpret those historical facts which otherwise would not be clear. Beyond this I have in some cases resorted to pure imagination in order to make unknown and unknowable history relate an ordered tale to the reader. . . . Adhering as closely as I can to historic fact so far as I can ascertain[,] I have added the fiction of interpretation so as to make a reasonable story. (I, 315–16)

Du Bois recognizes he is violating historical accuracy in order to present a thematic truth that is different from what a scrupulously empirical researcher would find. Yet, he also asks that these novels be taken seriously as history; for Du Bois intends his "fictions" as sequels to an uncompleted project, initiated with *Black Reconstruction* (1935), which was to write a history of America "with especial reference to the efforts and experiences of the Negroes themselves."[10] In the postscript to *The Ordeal of Mansart*, Du Bois writes:

> If I had time and money, I would have continued this pure historical research. But this opportunity failed and Time is running out. Yet I would rescue from my long experience something of what I have learned and conjectured and thus I am trying by the method of historical fiction to complete the cycle of history which has for a half century engaged my thought, research and action. (I, 316)

In short, then, from the beginning Du Bois was scrupulously aware of the capabilities and limitations of historical fiction.

The Mansart family represents less a group of average Afro-Americans than what Du Bois elsewhere called "the talented tenth" of their race, who were not necessarily leaders of their people but examples of the possible achievement. Thus, they can attain a freedom of thought, choice and action greater than that available to most of their peers; moreover, their family traditions, buttressed by middle-class standing, support the individual ambition of every Mansart. Tom Mansart, the first of the trilogy's protagonists, is a union leader and an elected member of the Reconstructionist legislature of South Carolina. On the night he is lynched, in 1876, his son Manuel Mansart is born. Manuel becomes, successively, a back country school teacher, the head of a black school in Atlanta, President of the Georgia State College for Negroes. One of his four children (or Tom's grandchildren), Revels, after his brief marriage to a white woman, becomes an eminent lawyer, a judge in New York City, and then a "fellow traveler" in Communist circles. His second marriage being childless, Revels and his wife adopt a son, Revels II, who kills himself while an airman in World War II. Douglass, the eldest son of Manuel Mansart, after brief employment with a black-owned insurance business in Chicago, becomes a wealthy Democratic politician in Chicago. His son is Adelbert Mansart. Manuel's third son, Bruce, is a college football star until he gets into a fight with a white man; the police put him in jail and subject him to a vicious beating. After several periods in prison, he dies prematurely of unspecific causes. The last of Manuel's four children, the sole daughter Sojourner, marries a rising young minister Roosevelt Wilson, who eventually becomes bishop of the [African] Baptist Church in Texas. Du Bois's technique as a novelist is to survey their careers in successive chapters, checking on the fate of each member of the Mansart family and, in effect, gauging the various possibilities they represent.

From the time that Lincoln's Emancipation Proclamation freed the slaves, the white landowner in the South believed that unless he "forced Negroes to work for nothing beyond the cost of their support, he faced financial ruin." (I, 140) So the landowners instituted the system of "sharecropping," where a tenant farmer borrows a plot of land, purchases on credit his seeds and supplies, and then tills the soil. In theory, the tenant farmer would pick the cotton, sell it, split the proceeds with the landlord, pay his debts to the store, and clear a fair profit. In practice, the landlord owns the only cotton gin in the sharecroppers' territory; so lacking competition in purchasing raw cotton he can offer them outrageously low prices. "Of course," Du Bois adds:

> The store prices are high. [The Afro-Americans] calculated that they paid 25–50% interest a year, and . . . it was well-known that the landlord and merchants down there didn't make money on the cotton except in very good years, but made it always on the store charges. The Negroes could seldom get a statement of their account, but simply a report of the goods purchased and the amount of money due them. (II, 264)

As the farmer could never pay off enough of his debt to receive a straight cash payment, the system kept him permanently in debt to both the landowner and the local store. Thus tied to his "benefactors," he was unable to set up his own farm, bargain his labor with another employer, or stray off to the cities.

No group within the South was at all disturbed about the Afro-American predicament. The planter class realized that unless black labor was cheap, American cotton could hardly compete on the world market. The poor white laboring class looked upon Afro-Americans as not only a potential competitor for the better jobs in the South but a threat to existing wage levels. Since neither group is willing to grant a black man any economic or social opportunity, Afro-Americans, dissatisfied with the subservience of the "happy nigger," learned that reliance upon either poor whites or wealthy planters would be hopeless.

Sociologically speaking, the American South portrayed in Du Bois's novel was not a pure totalitarian society, capable of regimenting every major aspect of Afro-American existence; rather, white power in the South is authoritarian, capable of thwarting challenges to its hegemony. Thus, an Afro-American in post-Reconstruction times who considered bettering his or her existence discovered that mobility was a road filled with perils, for the ultimate power of white society lay in the use of violence, both legitimate and illegitimate. Much of the law of the old South was designed "to keep the niggers in their place," while policemen in concert with the courts could employ an arsenal of misdemeanors to discipline all sorts of digression, ranging from looking too long at a white woman to setting up a competing business. Although whites accused blacks of incipient beastliness, the former so monopolized extralegal violence that black attacks on whites were almost an impossibility. Not only were Afro-Americans so intimidated that they scarcely acquired requisite weaponry and rarely organized any planned retaliations, but Southern whites also had greater experience in the use of violence. Moreover, the Southern courts, controlled entirely by whites, would always support a white person's testimony against a black's, no matter how patent the white person's lies.

In the opening passage of the novel, Tom Mansart, already a citizen of some standing, commits the heroic act of rescuing Mrs. Breckinridge, the plantation owner's wife, from a white mob about to attack a black meeting; but the white mob catches the horse-drawn buggy in which he is driving her away. Claiming that Mansart had abducted the white lady, the white men shoot him dead, despite her protests, and deposit his body on the doorstep of his house. None of the killers are ever prosecuted; and when Breckinridge later learns of Mansart's fate, she commits suicide in sympathy or remorse.

II

The trilogy shows how the superior capacity for violence makes individual reverse violence foolhardy and its success impossible. One autumn afternoon, when Manuel Mansart's State College beats Atlanta University at football and Georgia Tech triumphs over the University of Georgia, the celebrating crowds, led by their respective teams, accidentally encounter each other on a street in downtown Atlanta. "Southern tradition," Du Bois writes, "was that the colored people should always yield the sidewalk to the white; but in common practice, tradition was not always called upon to act." (II, 191) Bruce Mansart—the college president's handsome son, captain of the team, and hero of the day—steps to the side of the pavement without stepping off it to let the whites pass. When a drunken white shouts an antagonistic epithet, the white football captain and Bruce scuffle.

> It was then that the white police moved in, led by Officer Branigan, a fat and leisurely sergeant. As a discipline of Scroggs and a born "nigger hater," he realized that here was racial trouble where he need not hold his punches. Wildly the boy lunged and struck the officer square [sic] in the eye, and the large and rather corpulent man stepping back, stumbled and sprawled in the gutter.

His fellow policemen launched themselves on Bruce. He was pounded, torn, and thrown into the Black Maria which appeared with a shriek. A dozen black students were also arrested but none of the whites. Once in jail, Officer Branigan took off his coat, rolled up his sleeves, and with the help of his fellow officers beat Bruce until he was insensible. (II, 192)

The beating completely destroys young Bruce—damages his body and warps his mind. "There was a headache that never left him, always hurt, and at times changed from faint discomfort to a piercing flame that drove him half insane." (II, 143) Bruce Mansart drops out of school, moves away from home, intermittently corresponds with his family, goes to jail, enters the black underworld and dies at an early age. Du Bois, who continually portrays how evils in white society can corrupt pure Afro-American souls, makes it quite clear that this beating is the sole circumstance that initiated Bruce's demise. The ambitious Afro-American in the South recognizes that any success he achieves in life can be destroyed by white terror, acting within and above the law and without fear of reprisal; and no Afro-American, not even a Mansart, is important enough to be immune.

For similar reasons, group violence on the part of blacks produces only more massive retaliation from whites. In Mississippi, in 1919, writes Du Bois, an African-American assassinates a white man who had just raped the former's comely wife. Both the blacks are killed by the white man's companions; one of them is, in turn, shot by a mysterious unidentified black who happens to be in the area. At the same time, a black sets afire the house of a local small planter, and the latter's sons, in turn, raid and pillage the black homes in the area. The point of these exchanges is that the whites are always able to raise the level of the battle, initially through the superior recourse to, and experience of, the resources of violence. When he is informed by telephone of the disturbance, the state's governor sends five hundred white troops. Other whites, upon hearing of the fray, come to the scene armed and drunk. Over a thousand Afro-American "insurrectionists," both male and female, are arrested and placed in stockades. They are not allowed to see friends or attorneys, and they are assigned a "lawyer" who neither summons witnesses nor prepares a defense. Convicting them in a few minutes, the court sentences them to death or long terms of imprisonment. To meet black insurrection, Southern whites exercise both legitimate and illegitimate violence, both finally with the tacit support of law officials.

In another, more symbolic scene, Du Bois demonstrates that black insurgence over whites is, to the Afro-American, more of a dream than a possibility. In a rather clever vignette, Du Bois portrays Ms. Freiburg, Burghardt's predecessor as lecturer in current affairs at Atlanta University, informing her class of an event (the time is 1865) that went unnoticed in the local newspapers. "Yesterday Menelik of Abyssinia overthrew the invading Italian army of Audo and slew 25,000." Recognition of the possibility that black men could triumph over white in a fair battle prompts Manual Mansart, unaware that the class had ended, to dream of "The Citadel of Africa":

Over the black land streamed the dark thousands, grim and terrible, red-eyed and foamy at the mouth; with the vast bulk of the black Emperor Menelik riding ahead, plumed with lion skin and corsetted with steel. He saw that Italian host, proud with the axe and fasces of ancient Rome halt, shiver and then turning, flee like wild and hunted things down the gorge of death. (I, 129–30)

Freiburg awakes him from his reverie.

Beneath all relations between black and white in the South is an inequity of expectation that stems finally from inequality in the recourse to violence. A Southern white always addresses a black by his Christian name, while the latter is permitted to use only "mister" as a preface to a surname. When a black makes a promise to a white, the latter expects the vow to be fulfilled; but when Colonel Breckinridge, a man who purportedly takes pride in his "word," promises Tom Mansart that he will address a meeting of black workers, he shamelessly neglects his commitments without sending any advance warning or apology. Everywhere in the trilogy, Manuel Mansart continually makes and accepts promises that are betrayed by whites.

Nonetheless, despite terrible and arbitrary obstacles, an Afro-American in the South can attempt to escape the roles that white society assigns to him. He or she learns to avoid acts that might provoke white violence, even if they might save a human life. This is the lesson that the novel draws from Tom Mansart's heroic rescue and, conversely, the wisdom of those who do not come to Bruce Mansart's aid. The Southern black learns to suppress gestures that would seem to challenge the status quo; for it is Booker T. Washington and Tom Mansart before him, in Du Bois's novel, who pragmatically faced this situation by asserting that if the Afro-Americans temporarily denied their desire for social equality and the right to vote, then they would have a better chance at earning a decent living. It follows that Afro-Americans should avoid conspicuous alliances, whether with white liberals or within the black community itself; for such alliances might be interpreted as threatening the existing power structure. Finally they must avoid becoming too conspicuous or too arrogant about personal achievement; for the whites are capable of taking it away from them and summarily putting them in their "proper place." The novel shows how even the most successful Afro-American, such as Henry Jones, a doctor, is capable of inventing "the darky act" to meet a potentially uncomfortable situation:

> Once when he had driven through a busy intersection with his showy horse and carriage a policeman yelled at him angrily:
> "Hey, 'nigger,' where do you think you're going?"
> "Ah'm goin' right back t'other side of that street, Sah, and sit there twel you tells me to start again," answered Dr. Jones with a purposely exaggerated accent and a broad smile.
> The policeman guffawed, and Jones escaped arrest and fine.
> (I, 192)

In general, an ambitious Afro-American in the South would be wiser to climb within the black community than serving as an intermediary between blacks and whites. Jobs of the latter sort could just as easily be filled by white people, and if a black held one he or she would be under close surveillance of a white man and subservient to him. Mansart's predecessor as "supervisor of colored schools" was a man who had a position without power:

> In truth he was a sort of errand boy for the white superintendent and the go-between who made known decisions, especially unpleasant ones, to the colored teachers; . . . and despite his rather timid recommendations [,] he had not succeeded in getting a new school or improving facilities for the existing Negro schools in ten years. (I, 308)

When he dies, Du Bois writes, "There was no one to see him pass away." Afro-Americans in roles of intermediary power succeed in only two ways. Some are effective tricksters, like "the presidents of the colored colleges [who,] when they met one another, laughed themselves to tears at the experiences of making white morons do what they were determined not to do." (III, 11) Others work under authorities who are sympathetic to their work, and it was Manual Mansart's good fortune to have such a white backer as Arnold Coypel, the superintendent of white schools in Atlanta and later president of the state university.

However, if white men of much greed and little scruple envy black enterprise, they can marshal the power either to usurp it or destroy it. *The Ordeal of Mansart* tells of Ben Davis who ran the Negro Odd Fellows Clubs in Atlanta. Disappointed at not becoming president of the national organization, he throws the Georgia Odd Fellows into receivership and goes to white bankers for a loan against its extensive property. The bank appoints a board of white receivers who, in turn, borrow more money from the bank. "When, after years of litigation these assets were finally 'liquidated,' there was nothing left for the colored policy holders." (I, 281) As one of the white conspirators in this plot observes:

> Negro business without political power is silly. Remember what the city did to those Negro physicians and teachers who bought and built on Boulevard. They stuck so many laundries and factories under their noses that the property isn't worth today half what they paid for it. In Macon, I'm told, they put a white whorehouse in the center of the best Negro residential district. (I, 286–87)

Sometimes the procedure of takeover would be less open and more complex, although its method was the same—the collusion of white businessmen with the government. When Mr. Perry's Standard Life (Insurance) Company began to succeed conspicuously, particularly in buying property and financing construction, state officials found its reserves "to be impaired and it was necessary to increase the stock." (II, 173) However, white people rather than black purchased the new stock, and before long, "Its properties [were deeded] to a white company, the Southeastern Trust Company in trust. The Standard Life itself was merged with the white Tennessee Company [which] gutted the Standard Life of all its most valuable securities." (II, 173–74) By these machinations, it is implied, a successful Afro-American company could easily disappear into a white enterprise.

Those scenes that deal with the question of trusting white people become an implicit commentary on Booker T. Washington's ideas. Washington, one remembers, held that if Afro-Americans put in abeyance their desire for social and legal equality, they would have greater freedom to improve themselves economically. The point made in the novels is that Afro-Americans are economically insecure unless they know the law will defend their legitimate interests, and they will never influence legal processes unless they attain the right to vote.

In contrast, the only Afro-American institution in the South that has largely "escaped the daily dictation of the [powerful] whites . . . and the envy and interference of the poor whites [was] the Negro church, [thereby becoming] the most powerful organization extant among these people." (II, 241) Manuel Mansart's son-in-law, Roosevelt Wilson, becomes a minister in part because he hopes that immunity from white control will enable him to implement his activist sympathies. However, as a minister, he discovers that the Afro-American church has little real impact upon its membership and that it is completely ineffectual before white power. In one instance, Wilson is unable to remove a white-controlled house of prostitution from its site near the church; for not only had "Kent House" contributed generously to the church, but several of its black custodial employees were on the church's board of trustees. When one of Wilson's female parishioners sets fire to the house, Wilson cannot campaign effectively against the building's repair. Moreover, because Wilson is transferred to a new church every few years, he can never construct a lasting social program with any of his congregations; and as the bishop becomes less sympathetic to his work, Wilson receives progressively less attractive assignments. In response, he begins to have designs upon the bishopric for himself. Douglass Mansart, at Sojourner's request, becomes his brother-in-law's campaign manager; and without Wilson's knowledge, he bribes and cajoles the other ministers to effect Wilson's victory. Ashamed for a while of Douglass's dishonest maneuvers, Wilson still accepts the position; but as success dampens his reformist impulses and as the church organization misplaces and transforms his radical proposals, "The firm basis of conservative, respectable church life was not altered a bit." (III, 197) The African-American church and nearly all its ministers simply are not interested in advancing their race and even the most eager and energetic reformist ministers succumb to the machinery of accommodation.

Theoretically, a man forbidden to vote can express his political designs in extrapolitical activities, such as public petitions and demonstrations or, in the novel, bargaining with the powers-that-be. Some Afro-American leaders in *Black Flame* propose to politicians representing the poor whites that they consider an alliance with black labor to overthrow, in Marxist-Populist fashion, the connecting link between poor Southern labor and exploiting Northern money. The Populist agitator Tom Watson, in the earlier phases of his career, and his black associate Sebastian Doyle form the nucleus of such an alliance. Du Bois writes, "Watson and Doyle both attacked lynching; they denounced the Ku Klux [Klan]; they demanded the abolition of the convict lease system which was the modern slave trade." (I, 171) Frequently, Watson personally protects his black colleague Doyle from white threats and assassins.

However, their efforts inspire two enemies: opportunistic white politicians like Ben Tillman, ready to capitalize on the whites' fear and distrust of Afro-Americans for his own political success, and capitalists who recognize that such a revolution would end exploitation and decrease, if not destroy, lucrative profits. In Du Bois's interpretation, the forces of finance gang up against Watson's movement, first by preaching that "race difference must be emphasized and enforced by law." After interracial Populism earns a large following in Southern states, its enemies engaged in more underhanded and desperate maneuvers:

> Campaign funds poured in even from corporations in New York. Voters were threatened, intimidated, assaulted and at least fifteen Negroes were killed outright. At the polls votes were openly bought, forced, stolen, thus, the Georgia election of 1892 proved a farce, with terror, fraud, corruption and trickery. Federal supervisors under United States marshals attended the election in Augusta [for example], but could not prevent repeating, bribery, ballot-box stuffing, voting of minors and intimidation. The total vote in Augusta was double the number of legal voters. (I, 176)

Du Bois charges that although Watson's movement actually received a majority of the popular support, it was defrauded and gerrymandered out of its victory. Soon afterwards, the white powers reactivate their own wisdom, "Unless the Negro vote was legally disfranchised, the united white and black vote might be victorious over Big Business." (I, 171) In the end, the response to the potential success of interracial Populism is, ironically, laws that more fully segregate and suppress Afro-Americans.

After the Watson affair, Afro-American political activities focus upon regaining the right to vote. How does one obtain it? Only by persuading someone who is enfranchised that it is in his or her interest to give it to you. John Hope, the president of Morehouse College (and in life, Du Bois's closest friend), suggests that the most likely solution for Afro-Americans would be an alliance of "black and white labor in one movement for the uplift of the working class; we may beat back disfranchisement and restore the idea of democracy to the United States." (I, 294) In the trilogy's second volume, Manuel Mansart suggests to the poor white labor leader–politician Abe Scroggs: "Unless you eventually let Negroes vote for you, the employers will let them [the Negroes] vote for them [the employers] and kill the labor movement." (I, 184) Although Scroggs expresses a deep antipathy toward blacks, he admits the notion makes sense; for only a few days before (and several times afterward), Huey Long, a fellow poor white, had offered Scroggs the same argument:

> One of these days you have got to admit Negroes to unions and the polls. Unless you do this Big Business has got labor strangled. White labor will be underbid by black labor. In my state, I am going to give Negroes schools and I am going to let them vote just as soon as they want to. You've got to do the same thing here in Georgia. (II, 311)

However, Du Bois also knows that an alliance between Afro-Americans and any group of Southern whites would have a tenuous career; for the whites would enter it in the same spirit as Colonel Breckinridge's promise to speak at Tom Mansart's meeting—less as a recognition of moral and political principle or even a firmly bound promise than as an opportunistic gesture that could be suddenly rescinded for the same purely political purposes that originally motivated it. That is, the Afro-American right to vote was not per se respected; rather, one or another group would dangle the bait of voting rights only if it could believe (or, even better, be ensured) that the gesture would win black support. Later, the novel quotes Harry Hopkins as saying, "Huey Long is a good socialist and for the people, but first he's for Long and you can never tell where he'll end." (II, 334)

The novels make it quite clear that if Southern blacks were to obtain the right to vote, they would use it primarily on behalf of their racial interests. Du Bois refers to "an incident in Louisville where in order to issue bonds, in this case for school purposes, a majority of all citizens and not simply whites was required." The blacks discovered that the money would be spent almost entirely for white schools. Recognizing and exercising their power, "They proceeded to defeat the bond issue." (II, 110) Likewise, in Atlanta, "In 1919, the colored people organized and defeated a bond issue because they could not get the city to promise them new schools even if the bonds were issued." (II, 172)

The trilogy also portrays the radical possibility, historically slight, of the formation of all-black communities within the South. Du Bois traces the development and decline of the Afro-American settlement that sprang up in the Georgia and South Carolina Sea Islands after General Sherman opened them to free men in January 1865. Tom Mansart, among others, staked out a claim and tilled the land, becoming a moderately successful farmer, all with the truly benevolent aid of the Freedman's Bureau; but, "Suddenly, almost without warning, the government takes his little plantation and gives it back to its former white owner." (I, 30) Unable to labor under the farm's new landlord, Mansart drifts back to the mainland. Du Bois also praises the efforts of Isaiah Montgomery, who founded the colony of Mound Bayou in Mississippi. The project succeeded for a while, largely because of Montgomery's dictatorial control over his constituents and his scrupulous deference to outside white authority; but even at the height of its success, Du Bois remembers, "[Afro-Americans] whispered: what can a black man do in a white state where the blacks have no vote? Little or nothing." (III, 15)

Nonetheless, in the early 1950s, echoing Blessed Alwyn in *The Quest of the Silver Fleece*, Jackie Carmichael, a relative of the Mansarts (and, thus, part of the novel's collective protagonist), and his Danish-educated wife Ann, the granddaughter of Hiram K. Revels, the last black Senator from Mississippi, plan to convert his family's dilapidated farm into a communal settlement with farms, grazing lands for stock, some small industry, a school, and a hospital. "We are not fools; we know the opposition will be strong. . . . We are prepared for violence—we are going to be armed even to sub-machine guns." (III, 286) Although Du Bois never reports on the fate of their experiment, the final words about this ambition comes from Philip Wright, Revels Mansart's son by his first marriage (to a white woman): "Jackie and Ann, down in Mississippi, cannot exist as small farmers—they are manipulated by the white market, pawns of petty white politicians, under perpetual threat of the mob." (III, 344) The point is that in over a century the attitude of whites in the deep South toward independent black organization had not appreciably changed; whites still had the social and political power to hinder Afro-American ambitions for self-determination.

Within the South portrayed in *Black Flame*, the Afro-Americans' best friends are those whites who for various reasons are sincerely sympathetic to Afro-American needs and aspirations. One example is a Dr. Grogman (called "Crogman" in the opening volume) who has taught for forty years at Clark University in Atlanta. At age seventy-five, Grogman knows his university will die upon his retirement, for Booker T. Washington has ruled that industrial schools are more necessary than liberal arts colleges to Southern blacks. Another sympathetic white is Arnold Coypel, superintendent of Atlanta schools; for when the state wanted to appoint Mansart "principal" of the new state college for Negroes, Coypel insisted that Mansart's title "must be 'President' Mansart, not 'principal.' " (II, 100). In effect, Coypel selflessly mediates between the white centers of authority on one hand and Manuel Mansart with his program for black education on the other.

The sole group to be sympathetic, as a group, to the plight

of Southern Afro-Americans in the early twentieth century is
the idealistic, economically disinterested minority of Northerners,
"who recited the Golden Rule and the Declaration of Independence. They held high the tattered flag of the Abolitionists and
accused the nation of betraying freedom and democracy." Du
Bois adds that they were "the only Americans, at the opening of
the twentieth century, defending the real democracy in the United
States." (I, 228) Only a few of this group were so devoted to their
principles that they would selflessly act upon them; but from
these few come other benefactors, like Ms. Freiburg, who were
underpaid instructors in black Southern colleges. "Here [Manuel
Mansart, as a student] came into contact with a new kind of white
folks: Northerners, both men and women, as teachers. He began
to make a new category of whites." (I, 122)

Later, Manuel Mansart, as a college president, encounters in
Harry Hopkins what he considers the highest example of white
liberal beneficence; and Hopkins is also the first government
official to receive favorable portrayal in Du Bois's fiction. From
the opening moments of their meeting, especially when he asks
Mansart, "How the hell do you stand this South?" Hopkins, then
associated with the Red Cross in Atlanta, treats Mansart as an
equal and sympathizes with his compromised position as head of
an Afro-American college. When Franklin D. Roosevelt appoints
Hopkins to head government relief, first in New York State and,
after 1933, for the federal government, Hopkins initiates programs
that help save all the poor, both white and black ("now the most
miserable of the miserable"), from starvation. Hopkins emerges
in the novel as the first white liberal of power and importance
seriously concerned with Afro-American betterment, the first to
be aware that especially since "in existing jobs, Negroes were
being replaced by white workers," they more urgently needed
aid. (II, 341) He eagerly seeks out black leaders, even those of
more radical persuasions, for advice on administering aid and for
information on corruption or discrimination in the program; and
when Hopkins hears that Eugene Talmadge's Georgia was betraying the plan, he temporarily withholds aid from the entire state.

Du Bois suggests, too, that Hopkins, along with similarly dedicated liberals, initiates change in the federal government's attitude toward Afro-Americans. Harold Ickes, formerly president of the Chicago N.A.A.C.P. and Franklin D. Roosevelt's Secretary of the Interior, appointed as his advisor on Negro affairs Clark Foreman, a liberal white Southerner, who in turn gathered black advisors around him. Eleanor Roosevelt made Mary McLeod Bethune, president of Florida's Bethune-Cookman Institute, a frequent guest at the White House and her own personal advisor on Afro-American matters.

> Will Alexander, who had inspired the Southern race relations movement, and served in the Farm Security Administration, brought Negroes into advisory positions so that, in the end, Negroes of education and ability had some voice in the Attorney General's Office, the office of the Secretary of War, the Federal Housing Authority, the Office of the Emergency Management, the Department of Labor, the Youth Administration, and the Federal Works Agency. (II, 343)

Hopkins' influence also extended outside the government. His friend Sally Haynes, a social worker, reveals her essential sympathies in a crucial incident. In the early 1930s, as Du Bois remembers it, Haynes finds herself accidentally assigned to share a temporary hospital residence with a black woman. When the manager of the dormitory, a white Southern woman, apologizes for her "terrible mistake," Haynes dismissed the offending official with a glare and a curt reply. It is Hopkins, Du Bois believes, who shaped one side of President Roosevelt's political sensibility—the side that expresses a socialist's awareness that the government must aid the poor. (The other side is "the English gentleman" who refuses to betray his privileged class.)

Just as nearly all of Southern Afro-Americans' most sincere and effective white associates come from the North, so the North comes to represent for the Southern black a new life, offering more social freedom, more equity in the use of violence, greater opportunities for remunerative employment—more of the amenities that can make human life rich and real. The first migrant in the trilogy is Colonel Breckinridge's most loyal black servant, Sanford Breckinridge (in blood ancestry his first cousin), who in late middle age quits his job as the colonel's manservant to go North. "I've been honest, hardworking, and faithful to my trust as your records will prove. You've treated me like you treated your horses. You took no notice of me as a man and your closest living relative." (I, 107) The point made both by Sanford and, in his commentary, Du Bois is that the most intelligent and independent Afro-Americans in South Carolina should have gone North in the 1880s.

After the Atlanta Riot of 1906, in which a white mob with the aid of the white police looted and wrecked black homes and killed and injured black people for four days, Manuel Mansart's "one personal reaction from the Atlanta Riot and the industrial situation seemed to be escape from the South." (I, 273) However, just as he is prepared to accept a proffered job in Gary, Indiana, Arnold Coypel, the new head of Atlanta's schools, offers Mansart the post of superintendent of colored schools, along with this promise: "I am going to do everything that I can to see that the colored schools of Atlanta have a fair deal." (II, 23) Although Mansart's wife relishes "the idea of getting out of the South, of getting away from discrimination," Manuel accepts the Atlanta post, largely out of sheer altruistic responsibility to his mission as an educator.

The North, however, attracts Manuel Mansart's two successful sons, Douglass and Revels Mansart, both of whom find more social freedom and economic success than they could have achieved in the South. (However, Douglass's son, Adelbert, decides on his own initiative, for reasons not clearly presented, to attend his grandfather's Georgia College rather than a Northern school.) Upon his retirement, Manuel Mansart himself goes North, first to San Francisco and then to New York. Not just for the academic professional but even for the economically enslaved Afro-American sharecropper in the Mississippi Delta, the North becomes the most immediate alternative: "They escaped, by night, in swamp and river, by rail, where possible." (II, 276)

Although the Northern cities offer a freedom of movement denied the Afro-American in the South, they also present a different set of problems and a wider range of possibilities, both favorable and unfavorable. If the dream of personal success could be more easily turned into a reality, so more likely, too, were the nightmares of bottomless failure, social neglect, irredeemable indolence, unemployment without land, and even starvation. Speaking of the migrating Southern peasants, Du Bois inverts a favorite image of Afro-American folk poetry to warn, "At the gates of these [Northern] cities two veiled figures welcomed them—crime in crimson and disease in grey." (II, 276) Just as the average Afro-American in the North looks for saviors, so do members of the "talented tenth," like the Mansarts, sample various paths, in the interests both of improving their own lives and benefitting the lives of their people.

Douglass, upon his demobilization in 1919, had the choice of joining a Southern black insurance company with "a good chance [of succeeding] if he wanted to become a modern, well-paid business man" or realizing a dream of a non-Jim Crow life in Chicago. "He had glimpses in France," writes Du Bois, of "something of freedom without a color line; he had made up his mind that Chicago was a place where he wanted to live and work." (II, 164) To his bad fortune, soon after he arrives in Chicago he witnesses one of the worst postwar race riots. Disillusioned by the injustice he sees—more blacks than whites are arrested; likewise, more are convicted—he returns to Atlanta. His father, Manuel, wants Douglass to become a teacher and, eventually, his successor as the school's president. However, Douglass believes, "The only way of escaping the penalties of being black was to make money, and he proposed to devote his life to that." (II, 167) In the course of the novel he comes to represent the worst kind of self-made black politician-businessman—venal, semiscrupulous, opportunistic, unconcerned with the general plight of his race, and alienated from his sensitive son.

Du Bois treats the possibility of assimilation into white society not in terms of passing, as James Weldon Johnson did before him, but first of marriage with white Americans and then of social and educational integration. Revels Mansart, like his brother Douglass, is considerably less altruistic than his father; and upon his demobilization he vows to become a lawyer and a judge—to seek great success in the Northern white world. When a white woman named Mary Wright, who wanted "difference, adventures, a cause and a hero to lead it," flirts with him, Revels finds his first proposal of marriage readily accepted. Despite the passionate love between the young couple, the marriage was too visibly eccentric to escape public notice and, eventually, color prejudice in its cruelest forms. "Neither quite dreamed how far it could go in a case like theirs." Not long after their marriage, Revels finds a note that reads, "I'm leaving for good. It was impossible from the first." (II, 212) Years later, however, when he meets his son by Mary Wright, Revels learns that rather than departing of her own volition, as he had always assumed, she was abducted by her brother and his friends and committed to a sanitarium. At any rate, the point is that social pressures, from both blacks and whites, make intermarriage an experiment with little chance of success.

After he obtains his law degree, Revels has a parallel experience with partnership with whites, this time in the world of legal business. He opens a new firm with two fellow students, one a Jew and the other an Irishman. "They had gone into partnership because they were all in the same boat. The only kind of law practice open to them was defense of petty criminals." (II, 215) However, here too Revels encounters prejudice. White clients generally selected the white partners over the Afro-American; so that once Revels obtains a lucrative retainer from an East Indian merchant, his partners make a graceful exit.

When he fulfills his ambition and obtains a judgeship, Revels discovers that he is still not an integral part of white society–not even in what he considers to be the greatest city in the world and the freest in the North:

What galled and cut him to the bone was the fact that he was still an outsider; that always, no matter what his accomplishment or position, a colored man was not counted as a man. Club life in any great city is of tremendous importance, and this was denied Revels Mansart and it would be denied him forever. No matter what his accomplishment or character, one has simply to be told he's a Negro. That settled it. He was not black-balled. His name wouldn't even come up for consideration. (II, 231)

Here and elsewhere, Du Bois's characters separately ask the question of why any Afro-American should attempt to enter a community that refuses to accept him as an equal member.

The problem of assimilation is more complicated in the case of Jean Du Bignon. Born in New Orleans, of a strain initiated by the governor's concubinage with his colored housemaid whose children he claims as his own, Jean Du Bignon looked Caucasian. However, as she passed through Radcliffe for her B.A. and then through the University of Chicago for her Ph.D. in sociology, she resisted the temptation to be accepted as a white person and, instead, freely decided to align herself to the Afro-American community, eventually assuming a job at Mansart's college. Here the plot suggests that Du Bois subscribes to the white Southerner's contention that one's ancestry (here called "Negro Blood"), rather than the precise color of one's skin, defines blackness; and since Jean Du Bignon is an octoroon, her rightful place would be in the Afro-American community. An Afro-American white enough to pass should remain an Afro-American; refusing any other explanation, such as the importance of family ties, Du Bois would seem to espouse a kind of blood filiation.

Later in the trilogy, an Afro-American male looks upon marriage with a white woman as a debasement of his racial pride. Jackie Carmichael, growing up in Springfield, Massachusetts, and later graduating from Yale University, has an affair with an Irish girl. Some years later, soon after they become engaged, Carmichael breaks off the relationship. "The matter of interracial marriage bothers me," he explained. "We may look at it as a way of settling the race problem by letting the Negro race gradually be absorbed into white and thus disappear in America." Nonetheless, he adds, "That means that all which the Negroes as such had to contribute to this country would be lost." (III, 284)

Similarly, in his retirement, Manuel Mansart doubts the final purposes of social integration—complete assimilation of Afro-Americans into white American society. Sometime after the Supreme Court's 1954 decision he comments:

> If I had the power, I would postpone this disappearance of the separate Negro school. It was a noble institution with an heroic history. It could rebuild a people and a history.
>
> If, for another century, we Negroes taught our children—in our own bettering schools, with our own trained teachers—we would never be Americans but another nation—with a new culture. (III, 306, 317)

Later, in the concluding novel, when extemporaneously addressing a conference on the future of Africa and the black race, Mansart explains, echoing James Weldon Johnson's narrator, "Black Brothers, let us never sell our high heritage for a mess of such White Folks' pottage!" (III, 341). In the end, then, the book would appear to suggest that the fewer close relationships an Afro-American had with any white Americans—the kinder whites being better regarded as benefactors than close friends—the more successful he or she will be. How this segregation will happen in America Du Bois does not envision, nor does he deal with the question of whether Afro-Americans should create their own economy. Rather, self-segregation seems posited as a kind of general ideal, somewhat tempered by Du Bois's chronic ambivalence, noted before, toward interracial cooperation. The role of both legalistic reform and the moderate protest movement is deemphasized in this trilogy; for although Du Bois spent twenty-four years with the National Association for the Advancement of Colored People, particularly as editor of its magazine

Crisis, he refuses to show that the N.A.A.C.P. had much favorable effect upon Afro-American existence. After the Mississippi Delta Riot of 1919, mentioned before, during which blacks were imprisoned and sentenced to death without adequate trial, as Du Bois remembers,

> The new Northern organization, called the N.A.A.C.P., entered the case. It appealed to the Arkansas Supreme Court for a writ of *habeus corpus*, which the court summarily denied. Then, to the astonishment of white Arkansas, the Supreme Court of the United States allowed it. The fight lasted four years and cost over $50,000. On February 19, [1923], the United States Supreme Court reversed the convictions of the six men. (II, 272)

Some time later, the other convictions in the Mississippi case were also overruled by the higher court. Although the N.A.A.C.P. lawyers achieved similar successes over the years, including the decisions to end segregation in travel and education, these activities, though mentioned in the novel, are not credited to the N.A.A.C.P. Du Bois does however credit A. Philip Randolph's threat in 1941 of an Afro-American march on Washington with prompting Franklin D. Roosevelt to issue Executive Order 8802 to abolish discrimination in the defense program. "Franklin Roosevelt in this way secured the almost complete backing of American Negroes for him and the Democratic Party," Du Bois wrote, adding, "This was even more important than equal distribution of relief funds." (III, 182) Instead of documenting the achievements of the N.A.A.C.P.'s legal staff, Du Bois frequently illustrates the large impact the *Crisis* had upon lesser Afro-American leaders, such as the Mansarts.

In measuring Afro-American achievements, Manuel Mansart in 1939 finds justification for the gradualist ethic; but the character of his list suggests that here Du Bois may be employing irony to reveal Mansart's limited perception rather than expressing his own judgment. The catalogue of "achievements" appears, on closer inspection, a summary of tokenism—the principle that one man's (the token's) success should mollify the desires of the many:

> The N.A.A.C.P. still lives; there is one Negro in Congress and one state senator; there are 14 members of state legislatures and 12 members of city councils; there are artists like [Roland] Hayes, [Paul] Robeson, [Jules] Bledsoe and Marian Anderson; there are little theatres among Negroes in four or five cities and one in Texas; there are 19,000 Negroes in college and 2,000 graduates a year. In the courts there have been some victories. The wife of the colored congressman dared drink tea at the White House; and there are triumphs here and there in athletics. (III, 101–2)

Later in the trilogy Du Bois shows that although federal law has shifted more toward favoring Afro-American demands, American customs lagged far behind. Even the much-heralded federal Fair Employment Commission of the 1930s had only limited accomplishments. "The majority of the Negroes in America were still disenfranchised by law or custom or by fear of violence or denial of work." (III, 83) Representing a generation more than fifty years younger than Manuel Mansart's, Adelbert makes the novel's final judgment of gradualism: "The handful of leading Negroes were getting rich—the mass of poor Negroes were getting poorer." (III, 292) In short, for Afro-Americans as a whole, gradual reform offered only a limited accomplishment.

Coupled with this criticism of gradual solutions is an exploration of various more radical movements. One was Marcus Garvey's movement, characterized by an unnamed N.A.A.C.P. investigator, as "not so much the man as the message: a new black world over against the dominant white." (II, 87) The movement gained a mass following, which contributed money that Garvey wasted foolishly. After his Black Star Line went bankrupt, Garvey himself was imprisoned for using the U.S. mails to defraud. In Du

Bois's judgment, Garvey's ideas were as admirable as his impact; however, he lacked organizational talent.

> He aroused a consciousness of Africa and of the dignity of the black race among West Indian peasants and spread it in the United States. His thesis was based on independent statism for black folk. . . . His plans were balked by lack of any African base of operation and by his own ignorance of trade and finance. (II, 88)

Why such competent bureaucrats as Du Bois did not join Garvey can probably be explained by the fact that Garvey once called Du Bois "more of a white man than a Negro and [he] seems to be only a professional Negro at that."[11]

Nonetheless, the expatriation espoused by Garvey (although not one person emigrated under his auspices) appears in the novel as a feasible alternative. Indeed, soon after completing the trilogy, Du Bois himself emigrated to Africa, acquiring for the first time a formal membership in the Communist party, renouncing his American citizenship, and assuming the position of the director of the secretariat in charge of publishing the first *Encyclopedia Africana* that was sponsored by the Ghana Academy of Sciences. In the trilogy, Adelbert Mansart, dismembered of an arm in Korea and disgusted by what he considers "a war of whites on colored folk," returns to Chicago with a hatred of America so intense that his father, Douglass, furnishes Adelbert with sufficient funds to allow him to become a "remittance man" at the Sorbonne. There Adelbert becomes involved with some mysterious colored revolutionaries whose polyglot diversity is reminiscent of Princess Kautilya's crowd. Rejecting his father as "a white American making money, buying votes, using 'influence' as other Chicagoans did" and all that his father represents, Adelbert renounces his U.S. citizenship to marry a Vietnamese girl, a race movement organizer (the possibility that this union might be considered interracial never arises); and he accepts a commission as a French colonial civil servant! That position he views merely as a stepping stone to Ghana, "where we become

African." (III, 304) The novel clearly suggests that, for Adelbert, expatriation was a good, justifiable choice; but what may have happened to him in Africa is another question—left unanswered—because he never appears in the trilogy again.

Various countries of Europe are portrayed as possible havens. Although Adelbert objects to France as a colonialist nation, and he believes some French professors are too paternalistic toward colored people, he finds France generally free of racial discrimination and a congenial place to live. In England, Manuel finds that discrimination is more subtly unspoken, but still frequent. When invited to dine at a posh London club, he notices that a certain Sir Evelyn Charteris, who is invited to dine with Mansart's group, stiffens once he spots "the black face of Mansart" and, without a word, exits into the hall. "Manuel was not for a moment deceived," Du Bois writes, "Here was an imperial servant who did not eat with 'niggers.' " (III, 34) Later, Zoe Coypel, Arnold's daughter, tells Jean Du Bignon of the volunteers in the Lincoln Brigade: "I'm told the Negroes loved Spain more than they ever loved America, for in Spain there was no prejudice against their color." However, neither Russia nor post–Civil War Spain is considered in these novels as a possible residence of Afro-American expatriates.

Expatriation, however, is portrayed as an alternative viable only for certain individuals, for Du Bois's concluding novel looks more toward the Communist party as an organizational savior. The theme is foreshadowed first with contemporary references and then with historical parallels until, toward the end of the trilogy's final volume, it comes to dominate the discussion. In 1932, which emerges as the turning point not only of the trilogy but also, in Du Bois's view, of modern Afro-American history, Manuel Mansart reads Karl Marx's *Communist Manifesto*. To Arnold Coypel he comments, " 'I like it, but will it work?' " (II, 361) When the Communist party nominates an Afro-American, James W. Ford, as their vice-presidential candidate, many black newspapers come to its support. Du Bois quotes the Baltimore *Afro-American* as saying: "No white group is openly advocating the economic, political and social equality of Negroes except Communists." (II, 362) In 1917, Manuel Mansart had "cheered the October revolution [because] he remembered that the Russian serfs were granted freedom only two years before the American Negroes." (II, 43) Later, when Mansart visits Haiti, he hears of François Emile Babeuf and thinks favorably of this "menial servant, [who] preached Communism, freedom for the Blacks, and the unity of white and black workers. He organized the 'Society of Equals' but was executed in 1797." (III, 78) Both here and elsewhere in Communist literature, Bebeuf is cast as a precursor of Communist movements, a hero killed by the eternal enemies of the free workers–"the owners and merchants."[12]

After 1932, Communism becomes a more valid alternative for many of the Mansarts. Jean Du Bignon notices that only Communists came strongly to the rescue of the unjustly convicted Scottsboro Boys; and in the late 1940s she accepts an invitation to a World Council of the Partisans of Peace in Paris. There she finds herself agreeing with Paul Robeson when he declares, "My people will never fight the Russians who have outlawed race prejudice." (III, 250)[13] At the conference she discovers that, "So many other countries, new nations and little folk, Africans and Asiatics, seemed to place their hopes for salvation with Communism." (III, 252) Later, at the personal invitation of the writer Ilya Ehrenberg, she visits Russia briefly and returns home to Georgia greatly impressed. In 1952, she is indicted as an unregistered agent of a foreign (Communist) power; and although she is judged innocent of the specific charge, she uses the occasion to voice her sympathies "with the objects [sic] of Communism." (III, 265)

Revels Mansart, once he achieves his childhood ambitions, becomes more concerned about the future of his race; and one day, when his retired father Manuel is visiting New York, Revels takes him to a conference at the Cloisters in Manhattan. Various colored people are present—Japanese, Chinese, Africans (in an affair also reminiscent of the Princess Kautilya's dinners)—to hear a mysterious and unidentified speaker say:

> Against this [Hitler's Big Lie] we must set the promise of the
> Soviet Union never to hold colonies, nor to join with colonial
> imperialism, and to outlaw every vestige of color and race
> discrimination within its borders. (III, 166)

However, the alternative of this international alliance of colored people, abetted by Soviet aid, is undercut by a subsequent
conversation in which a Japanese agent asks Revels Mansart if
"American Negroes would be disposed to help Japan." Revels
replies that the Negro people so far have pinned their hopes for
achieving equality on the evolution of American law and custom;
and later Du Bois concocts two parallel, equally fantastic scenes
to show why Afro-Americans would have been stupid to align
with such foolish dupes as the Japanese. When the same agent
pays a call upon Adolph Hitler, the Führer dismisses him with
such vile epithets as, "Get out, you yellow dog! Do you think
I will even tolerate you Japanese monkeys in my backyard? Do
you think I am going to share my rule with darkies?" (III, 189)
When the same agent later visits Joseph Stalin the Russian is
portrayed, in sharpest contrast, as a genial and considerate host,
who personally offers hospitality.

In 1956, Manuel Mansart, just before his death, by now a
Communist in all but membership, tells an audience: "I therefore
greet that land which first enacted equality of the races—Russia."
(III, 340) Elsewhere in the speech he equates the yearnings
of the proletariat with those of Afro-Americans, to suggest
that the Communist Revolution will be in the name of both
underprivileged groups. Therefore, both Manuel and the novel's
narrator celebrate when they learn from a refugee rabbi, "Africa
is arising. The rape of Ethiopia is a thing of the past. The end
of white supremacy nears, and the beginning of a black world
looms." (III, 331) Finally, on his deathbed, Manuel envisions the
millennium:

> I saw China's millions lifting the soil of the nation in their
> hands to dam the rivers which long had eaten their land. I saw

the golden domes of Moscow shining on Russia's millions,
yesterday unlettered, now reading the wisdom of the world. I
saw birds singing in Korea, Viet-Nam, Indonesia and Malaya.
I saw India and Pakistan united, free; in Paris, Ho Chi Minh
celebrated peace on earth; while in New York— (III, 349)

He expires before he can complete his report of this vividly
detailed dream, but his reference to the Vietnamese Communist
leader Ho Chi Minh in Paris implies the parallel of a black
Communist leader similarly celebrating in New York, which is to
say America. As a political novelist, rather than a utopian one, Du
Bois offers paths, not blueprints. That is, he eschews constructing
a picture of ideal life in the future—indeed, conspicuously absent
from the trilogy are portraits of African-American life in Africa
and Russia; instead, it offers reports from travellers or statements
of natives. However, the novel's critique of the inadequacy of
other less radical alternatives—both in the South and in the
North—would make both Communism and African expatriation
novelistically "logical"—credible—solutions to the Mansarts'
Afro-American experience.

Indeed, rather than just a Communist takeover of America, Du
Bois would seem to be envisioning a threefold revolution whose
parts were probably independently conceived and are, therefore,
possibly contradictory, though each embodies an identifiable
historical trend. First is the rise of the independent African
nations, such as Ghana, and the fulfillment of the dream of Pan
Africanism.[14] Second is the spread of international Communism,
not only over all of Europe but to American too. Third is the Afro-
American rejection of less radical and less organized reformers.
However, proposition one could be undermined by proposition
two, unless Russia for some unlikely reason allowed Africa to
develop on its own. Proposition three is somewhat supported
by the suggestion that Afro-Americans are naturally socialist;
in contrast, capitalism is the white man's mode of economic
organization. (III, 340) At any rate, Du Bois's notion of the
great millennium will encompass all these tendencies; thus, his

polemical strategies are more effective at just suggesting the future, as he did, rather than attempting to illustrate it.

In the end, although Du Bois's novels were published over a span of fifty years, their attitudes on politics are nearly all of a single piece. In *The Quest of the Silver Fleece*, the possibilities of individual African-American independence within the South are tested and found wanting; yet opportunities in the North are hardly better. Among the politically favorable portraits are, first, the few kindly whites who teach Southern blacks and, second, the agitators for a well-organized communal settlement that would compete with the white South. In *Dark Princess*, not only the South but also the North is rejected, as the novel's protagonist expatriates to India; and the novel predicts that all colored people will claim as their own the land they now occupy. In the *Black Flame* trilogy, nearly all Afro-American possibilities in America are tested and, finally, rejected; and again expatriation, particularly to Africa, is favored, in addition to alliances with international Communism. Du Bois's novels, in addition to posing general questions, also define a range of options that Richard Wright and Ralph Ellison, political novelists both, subsequently incorporated into their own fictions.

NOTES

1. Elliott M. Rudwick, *W.E.B. Du Bois: A Study in Minority Group Leadership* (Philadelphia, 1960), 26.

2. Du Bois, "A Litany at Atlanta," in *An ABC of Color* (Berlin, 1964), 34–37.

3. Rudwick, *Du Bois*, 36.

4. For discussion of this concept, see August Meier, *Negro Thought in America: 1890–1915* (Ann Arbor, 1963), 197, *passim*.

5. See Francis L. Broderick, *W.E.B. Du Bois: Negro Leadership in a Time of Crisis* (Stanford, Calif., 1959).

6. Edward M. East, *Mankind at the Crossroads* (New York, 1923), 120.

7. Sterling Brown, Arthur P. Davis, and Ulysses Lee, eds., *The Negro Caravan* (New York, 1941), 141.

8. Harold R. Isaacs, *The New World of Negro Americans* (New York, 1964), 199, 226. W.E.B. Du Bois, *The Autobiography of W.E.B. Du Bois* (New York, 1968).

9. Isaacs, *The New World*, 195; Rayford W. Logan, *The Betrayal of the Negro* (New York, 1965), 343.

10. Du Bois, *Black Reconstruction* (New York, 1964), preface.

11. Rudwick, *Du Bois*, 218.

12. See, for example, Edmund Wilson, *To the Finland Station* (Garden City, n.d.), 67–68.

13. Marie Seton, Robeson's biographer, asserts that this popular version represents a misquotation. In fact, she writes, Robeson said, "It is unthinkable that American Negroes could go to war on behalf of those who have oppressed us for generations against the Soviet Union which in one generation has raised our people to full human dignity." Seton, *Paul Robeson* (London, 1958), 196–97.

14. See the enlarged edition of Du Bois, *The World and Africa* (New York, 1965), 263–338; and Du Bois, *An ABC of Color* (Berlin, 1964), 199–212.

four

Richard Wright

And in this lies Wright's most important achievement: He has converted the American Negro's impulse toward self-annihilation . . . into a will to confront the world, to evaluate his experience honestly and throw his findings unashamedly into the guilty conscience of America.

—Ralph Ellison, "Richard Wright's Blues" (1945)[1]

Unlike James Weldon Johnson or W.E.B. Du Bois, Richard Wright thought of himself as primarily a novelist. Although he also wrote some reportage and much polemical nonfiction, Wright used the novel form more frequently than his distinguished predecessors; and all but one of these novels treat the general political problems of Afro-Americans. Indeed, of the major Afro-American novelists, Wright has the largest body of creative work—seven novels and two novellas—and even more than Du Bois's fictions, Wright's several novels exhibit a conspicuous development in their political implications. Themes for collective action that are suggested in his earlier writing are modified or even repudiated in later fiction, and character-types portrayed as saviors in youthful works become false messiahs in mature ones. In effect, then, such later novels as *The Outsider* (1953) become commentaries on the politics implicit in the work written prior to 1946. The six serious novels can be divided several ways: three are about African-American life in the South—*Uncle Tom's Children* (1938), *Black Boy* (1945), and *The Long Dream* (1958)—and three about African-American life in the North—*Native Son* (1940), *The Outsider*, and *Lawd Today* (1963). In their discussion of the African-American attachment to the Communist party, two are essentially pre-Communist in outlook, *Lawd Today* and *Black Boy*, and two are explicitly Communist in sympathy, *Uncle Tom's Children* and *Native Son*; the remaining two are post-Communist. (Wright's seventh novel, *Savage Holiday* [1954], a facile work dropped from many bibliographies, has no relevance here, as it deals exclusively with white people.)

All but two of the novels are similar in styles of characterization and in plot, while certain details and events, such as postal employees and unpremeditated murders, appear in more than one book. These fictions generally portray average young African-Americans who pass through rather typical social experiences. In the early part of these novels, the predicament of the young man is evoked—the world into which he was born offers him small opportunity to define and develop his possibilities. Although neither creative nor intelligent enough to compose his own solutions or even to seek out alternatives, he considers other political choices as they are posed to him, either by accident, the workings of fate, or an outside messenger. One exception to this pattern, *Black Boy*, has a similar plot, but its narrator, like Wright himself, is more perceptive and intelligent than his other protagonists—indeed, the novel is a kind of portrait of the artist as a young man.[2] The other exception, *Uncle Tom's Children*, has a variety of plots.

The first of Wright's published books, *Uncle Tom's Children*, is actually a collection of novellas, along with an autobiographical introduction, that attains such a unity of theme and tone that many critics have classified it as a novel.[3] Indeed, its structure resembles that of *Lawd Today*, written about the same time and posthumously published as a novel, in that both offer a panorama of African-American life—the former in the South, the latter in the North. The book's theme is stated in the epigraph, which, because it is unidentified, seems to have been written by Wright himself: " 'He's an Uncle Tom,' which denoted reluctant toleration for the cringing type who knew his place before white folk, has been supplanted by a new word from another generation which says: '*Uncle Tom* is dead.' " As the elder Afro-Americans defend the advantages gained by subservience to the status quo, the younger generation favors alternatives; and the crucial actions of this book portray the experience and activities of this emerging generation.

The novel's opening section, a group of autobiographical vignettes, describes the system of power relations in the South: how whites keep blacks subservient through their control over the means of violence, both legitimate and illegitimate, and how older African-Americans, Wright's "Uncle Toms," help establish the threat of white violence in the minds of the younger generation. Wright remembers that one day he "found the gang to which I belonged . . . engaged in a war with the white boys who lived beyond the tracks. As usual we laid down our cinder barrage, thinking that this would wipe the white boys out. But they replied with a steady bombardment of broken bottles," one of which cut Wright's ear. (1) Returning home, he expresses his outrage over unequal weaponry to his mother, only to be surprised that she slaps him for not abandoning the fight. She imparts what Wright characterizes as "Jim Crow wisdom: I was never, never, under any conditions, to fight white folks again. And they were absolutely right in clouting me with the broken milk bottle." (2)

In the second vignette, likewise concerned with the theme of power, Wright describes how he learns that the white man extracts signs of Afro-American subservience in every possibly competitive situation. At his first regular job as a helper at an optical company, Wright, now a teenager, expresses an ambition to learn how the grinding machines work. In return, one of the two white workers falsely accuses Wright of failing to address his companion as "mister." When they pursue the point, refusing to accept either Wright's denial or his apology, Wright comprehends the hidden purpose of the incident and quits the job. "When I told the folks at home what had happened," Wright concludes, "They called me a fool. They told me that I must never again attempt to exceed my boundaries." (4) In another vignette, Wright, now a hotel employee, learns that the white nightwatchman can slap each black maid on the buttocks and then extract approval of his act from his Afro-American escort, that a black bellboy caught in bed with a white prostitute was automatically castrated, and that an African-American who failed to address a white man as "sir" was immediately vulnerable to retaliatory violence. Against all these affronts, the young black is supposed to do nothing except grin. This monopoly of the use of violence, Wright realizes, preserves social peace in the South. "Ef it wazn't fer them polices 'n' them ol' lynchmobs," a friend tells Wright, "There wouldn't be nothin' but uproar down here!" (9)

Other sections of *Uncle Tom's Children* describe similar incidents of violent exploitation of Afro-Americans. In "Long Black Song," a white traveling salesman rapes a nursing black mother without any fear of justice or reprisal. In "Fire and Cloud," white thugs abduct an elderly black minister and subject him to a beating. In "Bright and Morning Star," an authorized white posse attacks the mother of a black Communist and then captures her boy, breaking his bones and lynching him. In the ironically titled "Down by the Riverside," whose title comes from a folk song in which the narrator finds his love "down by the riverside," Wright's protagonist helps evacuate a flooded hospital and then rescues the children of the man he has killed; but rather than recognize the extenuating circumstances or bring him to a legal trial, white soldiers shoot him dead on the spot. In the opening story, "Big Boy Leaves Home," the protagonist kills a white man in self-defense. When a white mob finds his companion, they lynch him with sadistic pleasure; still unable to find the killer, they set his parents' shack afire.

In incidents such as these, Wright dramatizes his theme of differences between the generations: The parents accept the inequity in violence as an irreversible hardship; the younger African-Americans want to forge an alternative. In the opening vignettes, emigration to the North is presented as the best solution to black life in the South, as it was, in fact, for Wright himself. In a later section, while Big Boy and his friends are swimming, Big Boy remarks, "Lawd Ahm goin Noth some day. They say colored folks up Noth got ekul rights." (18) Later, as he runs from a white posse, Big Boy hides in a truck, and a friend drives him northward to safety. Thus, his adventures illustrate that violent retaliation against white attack can succeed, though the rebel would be well advised to leave the South, as Big Boy does, if he wants to save his neck.

Although going North remains an implicit alternative in the other stories, Wright is more concerned with exploring the possibilities for rebellion within the Southern system. In "Down by the Riverside," an African-American dubbed with the archetypal name of Mann wants to save his pregnant wife and their unborn child; so he hijacks a stolen boat to drive her to the hospital. When the owner sees the boat, he tries to reclaim it; but Mann shoots him dead. If Mann had not for humane reasons returned to the scene of the crime to rescue his antagonist's children, the story implies, he would have escaped completely. In "Bright and Morning Star," an African-American mother gains dignity by ridiculing the white men who threaten her with violence if she does not reveal the whereabouts of her Communist son. In "Fire and Cloud," Wright discusses the possibility of a mass protest rally. Here the story asks that readers identify with the predicament of the Reverend Donald Taylor, a prominent black minister and the leader of his community. Taylor recognizes that if he supports a Communist-sponsored parade, he could mobilize enough of his personal following to make it a powerful protest. At first, Taylor wavers before conflicting pressures: not wanting his people to become involved with the Communists, he is nonetheless fully aware that they ought to protest against their starvation. After the white city officials attempt to bully him into denouncing the rally and white thugs then beat him up for failing to take a public stand against it, Taylor wholeheartedly supports the protest march. Just as the parade is coalescing angry energies, however, the city's white mayor offers the crowd food if they return home. Wright's story suggests that in organized numbers there is political strength, bringing not only freedom from white intimidation, but also serving as an effective threat in winning concessions.

In "Fire and Cloud," Wright again poses the question of the identity of the African-American's real allies. When Taylor is limping back home after his beating, he passes a white church ministered by an acquaintance. "Yeah, thas Houstons church," he thinks. "Spose Ah go to Houston? Now, he's white. *White.*. . . . Even tho he preaches the gospel Ah preach, he might not take me in." (142) The whites who either bully the black minister or neglect him are contrasted with the two Communists who have come South to organize the protest. They not only preach racial equality in words, but they also act it in deeds. First, they address all African-Americans by their formal names. Though Taylor may be "Don" to the city's white officials, he is "Reverend Taylor" to Hadley and Green, who also promise to organize the poor white Southern workers behind the African-Americans, thus presenting a popular front not of blacks alone but all starving laborers—a move which, it is implied, confronts the real motives of Southern exploitation, motives that have more to do with capitalism than racial antagonism. Second, Hadley and Green, respectively, white and black, practice equality between themselves, sharing leadership and danger. Finally, in this story there is no suggestion that the Communists are motivated by anything other than altruism. Earlier in the story, they tell Taylor, still indecisive, "You know the Party will stand behind you no matter what happens." (123) The more the blacks see of Hadley and Green the less reason they have to doubt their claim. In *Uncle Tom's Children*, the only white people that African-Americans can trust are the Communist organizers.

In "Bright and Morning Star," there is a curious political note, rather confused, because either it is not intentional or Wright chose not to develop it. The white man who infiltrated the Communists to reveal its activists' names to the white Southern official has the peculiar name of "Booker." One implication here is that although Booker T. Washington and his followers pose as black radicals, they might as well be white men for all their political loyalties; a more basic corollary is that the "Bookers" of the South are not to be trusted by the young rebellious Afro-Americans for they will betray the cause of race advance just as easily as Booker T. himself did. Against the treacherous Bookers, Wright poses both emigration North and alliance with militant Communists.

In his second book of fiction, *Lawd Today*, written at approximately the same time as *Uncle Tom's Children* but not published until 1963, Wright explores the possibilities of African-American life in the North. Like *Uncle Tom's Children*, *Lawd Today* is constructed more as a series of vignettes than as a developed plot, to present a milieu, not dramatic action. Its principal interpretation of African-American existence in Chicago is conveyed in the novel's opening image of a black man running up a flight of steps:

> But somebody was calling and he had to go up. . . . It was hard work, climbing steps like these. He panted and the calves of his legs ached. He stopped and looked to see if he could tell where the steps ended, but there were just steps and steps and steps . . . he thought as he stretched his legs and covered three and four steps at a time. Then, suddenly, the steps seemed funny, like a great big round barrel rolling or a long log spinning in water, and he was on top treading for all he was worth and that voice was still calling. (9)

This passage describes not an actual event but, rather, a dream of Jake Jackson's, Wright's protagonist, who emigrated from the South because, as the novel later explains, "Chicago seemed like the Promised Land." (154)

What Jake discovered in the North is a syndrome of economic exploitation and indebtedness that bears some resemblance to slavery. "Each week the bills were mounting; each week he was falling further behind. . . . He owed so many debts he did not know which debt to pay first. . . . *What to Hell? What in the world can a man do? I'm just like a slave.*" (20–21) When Jake wants to take a short-term loan of $100, the interest, he discovers, is $20. Unable to find a way out of the debt system, Jake owes $500 at the novel's beginning; at its end he must pay at least $770. His salary at the post office is $2,100 per year, and his wife needs an expensive operation. Nothing offers hope, not even gambling. "He had been playing policy off and on for five years, but had never broken even. He was still behind. How much? He did not know." (42)

Although one character says, "If white folks could make us buy the air we breathe, they would," (116) the exploitation portrayed in the novel, particularly the con games, is largely practiced by African-Americans upon other African-Americans. Jake emerges as the prototypical dupe, always a sucker and rarely clever enough to suspect a swindle. In one scene, when he is about to be fired on a trumped-up charge, Jake is rescued by a telephone call from "Doc" Higgins, who succeeds in persuading his black superior to retain Jake; and in return, Jake pays Higgins $150 to fulfill the medicine man's demands. Completely unaware of the collusion that seems obvious to the reader, Jake is nothing but grateful to his savior. Later he picks up a light-skinned black woman at a dance; before long, she and her accomplice fleece him out of $100 he has recently borrowed. This time, as he protests, Jake recognizes, "He had been robbed, and these men were here to see that he did not bother Blanche who had helped to rob him." (180)

The issues of freedom and mobility take on paradoxical qualities in the novel. One of Jake's group asserts, "The white folks just ain't going to let no black man get to the top." (147) Nonetheless, the novel itself demonstrates that urban blacks possess a kind of lateral freedom—anything is possible within the Afro-American community, particularly if one is willing to resort to unscrupulous or illegal means. Jake, alas, is not intelligent enough to recognize this opportunity, and he never

considers striving for an existence better than his job sorting
letters at the post office—a job that another character compares
to being "like a squirrel turning in a cage." (131)

Still, alternatives do come to Jake in various forms. Doc
Higgins wants him to admire a white liberal benefactor, an
"old lady Lucy Rosenball [who] donated a million dollars to
the colored folks for a college down South." (58) However,
Jake discovers that the philanthropist had also donated "about
five million to build a hospital for stray cats and dogs."

The Communist movement is hardly a more compelling force.
At one point, an unidentified character admires "the Reds [who]
sure scared them white folks down South when they put up that
fight for the Scottsboro boys." (152) However, no one else in the
circle chimes in. Elsewhere, as Jake reads of a Communist riot
in New York, he explains to his wife:

> Now them guys, them Commoonists and Bolshehicks, is the
> craziest guys going! They don't know what they want. They
> done come 'way over here and wants to tell us how to run
> *our* country when their *own* country ain't run right. Can you
> beat them for the nerve of a brass monkey? I'm asking you?
> Why don't they stay in their own country if they don't like
> the good old USA? (32)

Later, when they meet a black Communist, Jake harangues him,
"Nigger, you'd last as long trying to overthrow the government
as a fart in a wind storm!" Continuing to "signify"—imply a
deprecating meaning—he adds, "Why can't you *red niggers* get
some sense in your heads? Don't you know them Reds is just
using you? When they tired of you they throw you away like a
dirty sock." (54)[4]

African nationalists are hardly more persuasive. When a group
of them hold a parade, led by a rotund, outlandishly dressed figure
obviously resembling Marcus Garvey, Jake and his friends are
more attracted by the drum majorette, whose beauty they find
just as compelling as her fancy stepping. Finally, throughout the

novel, which takes place on Lincoln's Birthday, Wright introduces snatches from a radio broadcast about Lincoln's life. Each time the outside voice enters the fiction, the story makes it quite clear that the radio program, which portrays Lincoln's achievements, bears little relevance to the present life of black Chicago. Moreover, the broadcast becomes an ironic commentary on the fact, illustrated throughout the book, that Afro-American emancipation from bondage is not yet complete. No solution proves acceptable to Jake; nor is his life in the North befitting of a "promised land." In commenting upon the fate of the humble, one character in *Lawd Today* says, "The only difference between the North and the South is, them guys down there'll kill you, and these up here'll let yu starve to death." (156)

With the publication of *Native Son* in 1940, Wright entered a new phase of his novelistic career, for the book was not only a critical success and a bestseller but such widespread response cast its author as a spokesman for Afro-Americans. Although he had disengaged himself from the Communist party's activities as early as May Day of 1936, he still retained his official membership in the party until 1942 and informal ties with certain Popular Front literary groups until 1944.[5] In June, 1941, for instance, he addressed the fourth conference of the League of American Writers on, according to Daniel Aaron, the Negroes' " 'dogged reluctance' . . . to believe in F.D.R.'s [war] propaganda."[6] Likewise, in *Native Son*, he wanted to show how the American Communist party could become a beneficial force in African-American life.

The opening scene of *Native Son* introduces both the milieu that shaped its protagonist, Bigger Thomas, and a symbolic event that foreshadows the novel's plot. The scene is the Thomas family's apartment, a dirty one-room place that costs its four occupants eight dollars a week. The time is the middle thirties, the setting, Chicago. No one in the family has full-time steady employment; they are unable to consider more suitable lodgings. As the family gets dressed, a rat slips through a hole into the room. Once the two boys, Bigger and Buddy, spot it, they push a trunk in front of the hole and ready their skillets to kill it. The rat runs furiously around the room, vainly attempting to find a place to hide. When Bigger kicks it, the rat slams into the wall, only to roll over, recover, and run some more, still unable to elude the violence that lurks over its head. When Bigger finally hurls the skillet, the rat collapses, dead. In this symbolic sketch, similar in purpose to the scene in which the land turtle crosses the road in John Steinbeck's *The Grapes of Wrath* (1939), Wright broaches the gist of his story. The rat is Bigger, but in his family house Bigger, in an ironic reversal, stands for the world's more powerful authorities.

In desperate need of money, Bigger organizes his friends to rob a nearby delicatessen; but just before they set their scheme into action, a relief agency offers Bigger a job as a chauffeur to the Dalton family. Though Mr. Dalton is a real estate man who owns much slum property, including, ironically, Bigger's own house, the landlord considers himself a devoted friend of Afro-Americans and contributes money to such Afro-American causes as the N.A.A.C.P. His daughter, Mary Dalton, whom Bigger is assigned to drive, is a student by vocation and a Communist by sympathies. On his first night of work, Bigger drives her to meet her friend Jan Erlone who takes them both to dine and drink. Everyone gets slightly tipsy at dinner, and on the way home they nip some more. When they arrive at the Dalton family home, having already dropped off Jan, Bigger finds that Mary is so inebriated that she has fallen asleep in the car. Unable to revive her, Bigger decides to carry her to her room. When he is putting her in bed, Mary's blind mother walks into the room to check on her daughter. Fearing the consequences of being discovered in her room, Bigger covers the girl's mouth with a pillow. Smelling the alcohol fumes, the mother condemns the girl for being drunk and leaves the bedroom. When the young man lifts the pillow from Mary, he discovers that she is dead from suffocation. Acting impulsively, he attempts at once to dispose of the body, carrying it to the basement and depositing it in the furnace. When Mary is found missing, the family's private detective, Britten, is put on the case. He suspects that Erlone is the perpetrator and has the police arrest him. Only later, when a reporter discovers bones and earrings in the ashes of the furnace, do the police come to suspect Bigger. He escapes into the black area of Chicago where he seduces and then kills Bessie, his girlfriend. Finally, he is caught by the police.

At this point Wright introduces political forces into the novel. The plot is structured to pose the question of who is the real ally of a victimized, but guilty, Afro-American whose unpremeditated crime is full of extenuating circumstances. Bigger's possible saviors become, in succession, the white legal officials, then white liberal philanthropists, then Afro-American religious figures, then the leaders of movements for black political rights, and finally the Communists. Each has a chance to come to the young man's aid; all but the last fail him.[7]

The officials of Chicago offer no help at all, instead exploiting Bigger's crime as an opportunity to terrorize the black community by rounding up several hundred suspects, by searching every Afro-American home "under a blanket warrant from the Mayor," by raiding the labor union headquarters, by encouraging the formation of white vigilante groups. (207) Once Bigger is captured, the coroner uses the inquest to confirm his guilt and also to implicate both his race and the Communist party. (273) At the trial, Buckley, the state's attorney, presses for a death sentence with the hope that a reputation for toughness will earn him popular support in his forthcoming competition for reelection—this move too exploiting a poor black for one's own ends. None of the white officials attempts to understand why or how Bigger committed the crime; nor, as Bigger's lawyer points out, do they offer any explanations more profound than that of innate depravity.

The white liberal philanthropists are deceived by their own good intentions, for as much as they regard themselves as helping African-Americans, they are unable to cope with the realities of the situation in addition to the limitations, if not hypocrisy, of their own involvement. Like Mrs. Dalton, they are interested in African-Americans in general but blind to the existence of actual individuals. With cutting irony, Wright portrays Mr. Dalton saying of his wife, "She's blind. She has a very deep interest in colored people." (41) The money they give to African-Americans does little to alleviate distress; for instance, the $5 million they donate to black colleges will produce diplomates for a white world that is, like Mr. Dalton itself, not at all eager to hire black college graduates. (278) Similarly, the ping-pong tables that Mr. Dalton donates to boys' clubs do nothing to change the fact that Bigger's gang planned their robberies there. (301) "Will ping-pong keep men from murdering?" Bigger's lawyer asks. Later, the lawyer explains that the Daltons donate to Afro-American charities to assuage their guilt over charging exorbitant rents for substandard housing. (278) Moreover, once they are made aware that the "terrible conditions under which the Thomas family lived" may have indirectly contributed to the formation of Bigger's character, Mr. Dalton vehemently refuses to "atone for a suffering I never caused." (251) Likewise, Mrs. Dalton insists to Bigger's mother, "I did all I could when I wanted to give your boy a chance in life," (256) and she thereby washes herself of any complicity.

Afro-American political leaders offer no succor to the victimized black. Bigger understands they would rather forget that Afro-American criminals exist. "They say," Bigger explains, "guys like me make it hard for them to get along with white folks." (303) Moreover, even before his crime, Bigger knew that Afro-American leaders would offer no aid to an unimportant black like himself. "They wouldn't listen to me," he says. "They rich, even though the white folks treat them almost like they do me." (303) Only at election time are they concerned about Bigger; then they encourage the twenty-year-old to lie about his age and receive five dollars for voting. When asked whether he thought participating in electoral politics could get him anything, Bigger replies, "It got me five dollars on election day." (303) Otherwise, Afro-American politicians do nothing to alleviate Bigger's troubles.

A more sustained attempt to help Bigger comes from Afro-American religion, but it too is unable to make sense of his predicament or give him hope. Soon after Bigger is imprisoned, the Reverend Mr. Hammond, the pastor of his mother's church, comes to his cell. After asking the Lord to forgive his wayward son, Hammond attempts to attribute the cause of Bigger's crime to Original Sin. He envisions Bigger repeating Adam's crime of eating of the tree of knowledge; and for this, God has cast Bigger "outta the garden." Jesus, in Hammond's story, has shown man how to live under the yoke of sin. "Jesus let 'em crucify 'im, but his death wuz a victory. He showed us tha' t' love in this worl' wuz t' be crucified by it. This worl' ain't our hom'. Life every day is a crucifixion." The only way out of this predicament is, "Be like Jesus. Don't resist." To transform the acceptance of misfortune into a victory, "You gotta b'lieve tha' Gawd gives eternal life th'u the love of Jesus." (243) Or, only a belief in Jesus and an afterlife can redeem a life of suffering. Although Bigger finds himself unable to respond to Hammond, he does not object when the preacher puts a wooden cross around Bigger's neck. At the coroner's inquest, Bigger's mother repeats the preacher's offer of salvation through religion, but to this plea Bigger can only reply, "Forget me, Ma," and offer his hand. "Knowing," Wright comments, "that his heart did not believe, knowing that when he died, it would be over, forever." (255)

As he is taken from the inquest back to the jail, Bigger sees a flaming cross on top of the building across the street and then recognizes the double symbolism of the cross around his neck. "That cross was not the cross of Christ, but the cross of the Ku Klux Klan," Wright comments. "He has a cross of salvation around his throat, and they were burning one to tell him that they hated him!" Feeling that the black preacher had betrayed him by foisting a symbol of the white man's religion on him, Bigger rips the cross from his neck and throws it away. (287) Later, when his lawyer asks Bigger if he were ever religious, the young man replied, "When I was little. But that was a long time ago." He stopped going to church, he explained, when he discovered, "There was nothing in it. Aw, all they did was sing and shout and pray all the time. And it didn't get 'em nothing. All the colored folks do that, but it don't get 'em nothing." (301)

From their first appearance in the book, it becomes clear that the Communists are Bigger's truest friends. Jan Erlone, the young Communist organizer, treats him as an equal. Unlike the Daltons, he does not use simplified, condescending English to talk to Bigger; and he also asks Bigger to address him as "Jan," instead of "Sir." When Bigger does not accept this privilege, Mary Dalton, Jan's girlfriend, reassures him, "Jan *means* it." (68) Moreover, when Jan decides he wants to take the wheel of the Dalton car, he has Bigger sit beside him in the middle of the front seat, not in the back, thereby sandwiching the young black between Mary and himself. Even when Jan leaves the car, Mary stays in the front seat. Furthermore, once they open the bottle of rum, Bigger sips from the same spout. Although the motives behind their sympathetic gestures may be as perfunctory in quality as Mr. and Mrs. Dalton's condescension (and Mary's pronouncements more saccharine than Jan's), they act toward Bigger as though he were an equal.

Once Bigger is indicted, the Communists are the only group in society to show real compassion toward him; for despite the fact that Bigger had killed Erlone's girlfriend and then attempted to frame him as Mary's murderer, Jan still goes to Bigger's aid. Just after the Reverend Mr. Hammond has vainly attempted to save Bigger's soul, Jan confesses that he, as a member of white society, is partly responsible for the murder Bigger has committed and, thus, partly guilty of it too. In recompense, Jan asks to take responsibility for Bigger's legal defense. After brief indecision, Bigger agrees: "He looked at Jan and saw a white face, but an honest face. Jan had spoken a declaration of friendship that would make other white men hate him. For the first time in [Bigger's] life a white man became a human being to him." To this recognition, Wright adds, in cutting mockery of the minister, "The word has become flesh." (246)

The second sympathetic white figure is Boris I. Max, the Communist lawyer who takes on Bigger's case. Max exhibits a sincere interest in Bigger's personal welfare—a tie indicated

symbolically when he addresses Bigger as "son," and thereby
not only establishes a more intimate relation but differentiates
himself from both Mr. Buckley and the Daltons who call him
merely "boy." Also, he converses with his client not as a ward
assigned by the court but as a fellow human being; and for his
empathy, Bigger after the trial responds with sincere gratitude,
"You asked me questions nobody ever asked me before. You
treated me like a man." (354) In addition, Max sloughs off the
warning of the state's attorney that he will hurt his legal reputation
by defending an African-American whom the press and public had
already judged as vicious and guilty. Admittedly, in the course
of the trial, Max sometimes seems more eager to condemn the
white society that he regards as creating Bigger than in saving
Bigger's neck. "If I can make," he rationalizes, "the people of
this country understand why this boy acted like he did, I'll be
doing more than defending him." (248) Nonetheless, although
Max reveals his tangential motives, he still does more to defend
Bigger than anyone else in the novel.

Unlike the white liberal philanthropist, the public officials, both
white and black, and the black preacher, Max refuses to accept
Bigger as a "demented savage," to quote prosecutor Buckley's
phrase. (346) He attempts a rational explanation of why Bigger
killed, and this forms the basis of his defense of Bigger's character
and his plea for clemency. Max argues that the crime was caused
not by Bigger but by the conditions that produced him—that, as
Max puts it, "His crime existed long before the murder of Mary
Dalton. Though this crime was accidental, the emotions that
broke loose were *already* there." Thus, "the accidental nature
of his crime took the guise of a sudden and violent rent in the
veil behind which he lived." (330) With different metaphors,
Max argues that because a minority group is oppressed, a new
"form of life . . . has grown up here in our midst that puzzles
us, that expresses itself, like a weed growing from under a stone,
in terms we call crime." (303) Executing Bigger will not get at
the root causes; if anything, by creating resentment, it will fan
hidden flames that may again burst into crime.

From these statements follows a political thesis that remains merely implicit in the novel—that Communist victory in America will solve the Afro-American problem, for only the Communists will radically change the social conditions and thus effectively eradicate the causes of crime. Such superficial allies as the white philanthropists and the black political leaders are too committed to the present white-controlled power structure to have any sympathy for radical change. As for the preachers, their obsession with otherworldly matters makes them politically impotent. So only the Communists can engineer the social transformations that will enable African-Americans to thrive in America.

In his next major book, *Black Boy*, Wright recapitulates some of the experience he describes in "An Autobiographical Sketch" that opened the earlier *Uncle Tom's Children*; in fact, whole passages from the earlier book are interspersed verbatim in *Black Boy*. However, whereas the earlier book focuses quite clearly upon inequities in the practice of violence, *Black Boy* treats a broader range of Southern experiences that are less specific than typical in emphasis, making the book closer to generalized fiction than a strictly personal record. Here Wright becomes more clear and specific about the possibilities that the South affords as well as his personal reasons for rejecting them.

Because alternatives are not immediately obvious to young Richard, his first choice is to accept the social role that empowered whites create for him; thus, his early years are spent discovering the boundaries of possible action. From the moment he first learns to evaluate life about him, young Wright is skeptical about Afro-American existence in the South. Looking at the poverty of his own honest, hardworking family, he concluded that good intentions did not reap their just rewards. His family was so poor that Wright did not have enough clothes to attend school. Once his parents separate, the burden becomes greater, neither one being able to cope with the South alone. In his father, young Wright sees the vanity of working hard within the Southern system that in *12 Million Black Voices* (1941) he described as enslavement to cotton, which "*is* a queen, not a king. Kings are dictatorial; cotton is not only dictatorial but self-destructive, an imperious woman . . . who is driven by her greedy passion to bear endless bales of cotton." (38)[8]

Describing his father as a withered man who had deserted his family twenty-five years before, Wright presents a current image to suggest an earlier one of a man who had not yet succumbed to the queen:

> [He was] standing alone upon the red clay of a Mississippi plantation, a sharecropper clad in ragged overalls, holding a muddy hoe in his gnarled, veined hands. . . . His soul was imprisoned by the slow flow of the seasons, by wind and rain and sun, . . . how chained were his actions and emotions to the direct, animalistic impulses of his withering body. (30)

Wright recognizes that his father's footsteps offer a path that the son had to reject: "I could see a shadow of my face in his face; . . . there was an echo of my voice in his voice." (30) Shadows and echoes as disintegrated outlines of wholes that were once solid suggest that the Southern system reduces man to a skeletal existence. Wright's main reason for rejecting the South is the unlikelihood of an African-American pursuing any career other than menial laboring or business that thrived on the exploitation of other African-Americans, such as insurance or undertaking.

From a very early age, he recognizes that his immediate Mississippi milieu is not sympathetic to intellectual or artistic pursuits. When he was about eight years old, he wrote an innocuous, sentimental story "of an Indian maiden, beautiful and reserved, who sat alone upon the bank of a still stream." (105) After reading his first creative work with pleasure, young Richard wondered to whom he would show it: "Not my relatives; they would think I had gone crazy." Reading it aloud to a young woman who lived next door, he discovers, "She smiled at me oddly, her eyes baffled and astonished." (105) A few years later, after writing another story that he entitled, "The Voodoo of Hells Half-Acre," he discovers that, "My schoolmates could not understand why anyone would want to write a story. The mood out of which a story was written was the most alien thing conceivable to them." (146) When he explains to his grandmother how he imagined the story, she insists that such a self-inspired creation is "the Devil's work." His mother, possessed of a more secular and practical cast of mind, argues that if Richard continues to write fiction, any kind of fiction, most people would identify him as "weak minded. Suppose the superintendent of schools would ask you to teach here in Jackson, and he found out that you had been writing stories?" (147) His Uncle Tom, contemptuous of his nephew's effort, commented that the fantasy lacked a point; his Aunt Addie blamed it all on his upbringing. When the story is published in the local newspaper, no one, aside from the editor, appreciates it. From these and similar experiences, Wright concludes: "My environment contained nothing more alien than writing or the desire to express one's self in writing." (105)

By observing the manner of his Uncle Tom, especially after the latter moves into the top floor of the Wright house, young Richard understands that even a semi-intellectual profession like school teaching would not suit an honest young African-American, for the teacher was required to play a petty role in Southern society. Once Uncle Tom asks him for the time of day, young Richard, impatient, gives him a straight answer, only to find his uncle so offended by explicitness that he wants to whip the boy. At first Richard is puzzled, "I did not feel that I had given him cause to say I was sassy. I had spoken to him just as I spoke to everybody." (138) Then he realizes that because Uncle Tom did not approve of his "tone," the old man "was going to teach me to act as I had seen the backward black boys act on the plantations, was going to teach me to grin, hang my head, and mumble apologetically when I was spoken to." (138) Here Richard recognizes that the black schoolteacher's main function is not to tell the truth about the world or to reveal the possibilities of life but to inculcate in young Southern African-Americans the ways of best serving their white masters. After he retired from teaching, Tom found an occupation of, it seems, equivalent social status and, it follows, equivalent pedagogical impact—repairing chairs. Asserting his own independence, young Wright rejects his uncle's example, "Your life isn't so hot that you can tell me what to do. Do you think I want to grow up and weave the bottoms of chairs for people to sit in?" (140)

As the maturing African-American perceives the discrepancy between the possibilities of life and the restrictions of the South, the system encourages him or her, as the novelist Ralph Ellison wrote in a critical article, to "perpetually resolve the resulting conflicts through the hope and emotional catharsis of Negro religion."[9] The older generation takes upon itself the task of inculcating the young with religious devoutness; but in reaction, each successive younger generation becomes less fanatical about religion than its elders. Wright's mother, for instance, departed from the home of his grandmother, because, he remembers:

> She had grown tired of the strict religious routine of Granny's home: of the half dozen or more daily family prayers that Granny insisted upon, her fiat that the day began at sunrise and the night commenced at sundown, the long, rambling Bible readings, the individual invocations at each meal. (52)

Religion has even less effect, in turn, upon young Richard. When his mother becomes severely ill, he goes to live with his grandmother, who makes him observe the strict rules of the Seventh-Day Adventists. When he attends religious school, he discovers that he is different from the prematurely repressed religious children whom he envies not at all. "These boys and girls were will-less," he remembers, "their speech flat, their gestures vague, their personalities devoid of anger, hope, laughter, enthusiasm, passion or despair." He discovers the church's impractical ways of dealing with reality through its choice of recreation. Baseball, marbles, boxing, and competitive track were taboo, but not "pop-the-whip" in which a chain of handlocked children would run left and right as fast as possible. When this human whip was, so to speak, popped, the end child is propelled, usually off the ground and through the air. "It would have been safer for our bodies and saner for our souls," Wright judges, "had she urged us to shoot craps." (96)

At the heart of Wright's rejection of religion was an indifference to the rituals of Christianity. Instead of thinking about the content of the prayers his grandmother imposed four times a day, young Richard becomes more preoccupied with his sore knees and devises a method of "kneeling that was not really kneeling" (197) At all-night prayer sessions, he easily drops off into sleep. Wright's negative experiences give him a purely worldly orientation that prevented any sympathy for religion. For instance, he finds a married member of the church choir more attractive and stimulating than the songs she sang. Even when he accepts baptism for the sake of appeasing his ailing mother, religion has no effect upon him. "The Bible stories seemed slow and meaningless when compared to the bloody tinder of pulp narrative. And I was not alone in feeling this; other boys went to sleep in Sunday school." (136) Each succeeding generation, it is again implied, will find religious solutions to Afro-American dilemmas less adequate than its predecessor found them.

In *Black Boy* Wright is again concerned with the role of violence in enforcing Afro-American subservience in the South. From his earlier *Uncle Tom's Children* he takes the vignette of the black hotel waiter who is killed for "fooling with a white prostitute," as well as the autobiographical sketch in which he is forced out of his job at the optical factory. However, in this later work, Wright emphasizes how African-Americans themselves accept and reinforce the white man's authority. The regular punishment for any misstep by a young black boy is a beating from his parents, a beating that serves as a sample of what he might encounter if whites discovered his crime and is, thus, often "administered for the child's own good."[10] When young Wright is rebellious in religious school, his Aunt Addie attempts to whip him; for making a profane remark in his grandmother's presence, he is struck with a wet towel. Always he is warned that white men would inflict worse harm. "White men have guns and the black men don't," his mother tells him. (52)

Since the life of menial labor brings no worthwhile rewards for endless toil, since no African-American can become a skilled laborer in the South, since self-expression is condemned by both races, since religion offers no real salvation to Afro-Americans' daily troubles, since the repressive violence is enforced by whites and reinforced by blacks, life in the South, says Wright, offers nothing of value to the sensitive and honest young African-American free enough to choose his or her own destiny. Since change within the South seemed beyond imagination, emigration to an area with less social control and greater personal opportunity is the only feasible solution.

> I was leaving without a qualm, without a single backward glance. The face of the South that I had known was hostile and forbidding, and yet out of all the conflicts and the curses, the blows and the anger, the tensions and the terror, I had somehow gotten the idea that life could be different, could be lived in a fuller and richer manner. My mood was: I've got to get away; I can't stay here. (226)

In the North, by contrast, he expects to find freedom that will allow him to shape his own existence:

> The pressure of Southern living kept me from being the kind of person that I might have been. I had been what the surroundings had demanded, what my family—conforming to the dictates of the whites above them—had exacted of me, and what the whites said that I must be. I was leaving the South to fling myself into the unknown, to meet other situations that would perhaps elicit from me other responses. And if I could meet enough of a different life, then perhaps, gradually and slowly, I might learn who I was, what I might be. I headed North, full of a hazy notion that life could be lived with dignity, and that if men were lucky in their living on earth they might win some redeeming meaning for their having struggled and suffered here beneath the stars. (228)

So, in *Black Boy* Wright makes clearer the same hope expressed several years before in *Uncle Tom's Children*, a hope that he undercut in the description of Northern life in *Lawd Today* and *Native Son*. In Wright's intellectual development, *Black Boy* represents a turning away from the solutions to Afro-American life posited in *Native Son* back to a more basic notion—essentially pre-Communist in the introductory scheme—that if the individual African-American is to thrive, he must leave the South. In Wright's changing politics, this fictionalized autobiography becomes a stopgap in which old themes are reinforced and new problems remain untouched.

In the same year that he published *Black Boy*, 1945, Wright contributed a first-person narrative of his experiences in Chicago to the second annual anthology of recent American writing edited by Edwin Seaver, *Cross-Section*; and this fragment was subsequently included in the posthumously published collection of Wright's short fiction, *Eight Men* (1961). Unevenly written and rather inscrutably structured, "The Man Who Went to Chicago" was initially part of the material cut from the final third of *Black Boy*'s original manuscript. The excuse given at the time by his publisher was a wartime paper shortage, but Wright suspected insidious Communist influence.[11]

Essentially, "The Man Who Went to Chicago" presents a debate over whether life in the North was really better than that in the South. On the one hand, Wright in the North admires the large number of decent liberal whites, especially Jews, who do not exercise inhumane authority or extract submissiveness in every encounter with a black. When applying for a job at a Jewish delicatessen, Wright is hired as soon as he announces he's from Tennessee, for the owner's brother-in-law once worked in that state. When Wright skips a day of work and offers a preposterous excuse, this boss accuses him of lying. Though Wright denies the perfidy, his boss replies kindly, "I know you're lying, but I don't care, Rich." (*Eight Men*, 166) To their sentiment and generous example, Wright responds incredulously. "He never had encountered anything like that from whites before. A Southern white man would have said: 'Get the hell out of here.' Or 'all-right, nigger, get to work.' It dawned on me that they were trying to treat me as an equal." At a later job as a cafe dishwasher, Wright discovered that white waitresses would sometimes need to squeeze against him to get to the coffee machine. In contrast to these women who were "relatively free of the heritage of racial hate," Wright thinks of a Southern girl who, had she "wanted to draw a cup of coffee, . . . would have commanded me to step aside so that she might not come into contact with me." (167) Because the heirs of the white slavocracy have such little power there, the North, particularly its cities, offers African-Americans a freedom of movement and a freedom from abuse incomparably greater than the South.

On the other hand, greater freedom of action does not bring unlimited opportunities; and the North, because of its uneven patterns of racial discrimination (both implicit and explicit), makes African-Americans insecure in their freedom. Wright suggests that discrimination is particularly pernicious when it leaves blacks unsure of both their place and the demands upon their behavior and response.

> I wondered if there had ever been in all human history a more corroding and devastating attack upon the personalities of men than the idea of racial discrimination. I would have agreed to live under a system of feudal oppression, not because I preferred feudalism but because I felt that feudalism made use of a limited part of a man, defined man, his rank, his function in society. (163)

From observing the Afro-American experience in the North, Wright adds, "I was learning that perhaps even a kick was better than uncertainty." (163) With this passage, he undercuts the solution posited at the end of *Black Boy*.[12]

The freedom of the North also allows unscrupulous African-Americans, already noted in *Lawd Today*, to assume a role that in the South was monopolized by whites, that of exploiter of

Afro-American ignorance. When he takes a job as an insurance salesman, Wright discovers this at first hand, selling to illiterate blacks insurance policies that "carried clauses severely restricting their benefit payments." Moreover, many insurance men, including Wright, often take sex in lieu of regular payment or, more viciously, extract sexual humiliation before they would pay the claims to which a black woman was entitled. At other times, agents would switch an old policy for a new one "which had an identical face but carried lower payments." (178) Most other Afro-American businessmen, Wright implies, are no more scrupulous.

No matter how much he criticizes Afro-American life in the North, Wright still cannot argue that African-Americans should return to the South with its orderly, stable system of servitude. Instead, he lifts the problem of Afro-American existence above the level of sectional choice into the realm of national attitudes, accusing America of failing to think sufficiently about the minority within its midst. "For White America to understand the significance of the problem of the Negro will take a bigger and tougher America than any we have yet known. I really do not think that America, adolescent and cocksure, a stranger to suffering and travail, . . . is ready to probe into its most fundamental beliefs." (170) Most skeptical readers, among them this writer, would probably believe that Wright has here moved beyond politics not into philosophy but into exhortatory platitudes, where all real questions dissolve into words. Wright deals honestly with the problems of North versus South, but he gropes for an answer surer than an ambiguous one.

The year before both *Black Boy* and "The Man Who Went to Chicago" were released Wright published two lengthy pieces— one an autobiographical narrative, *I Tried To Be a Communist*, which can likewise be understood as fiction; the other his best single piece of imaginative writing, *The Man Who Lived Underground*, which was also reprinted in *Eight Man*. When read together, these become a turning point in the development of his fictional rendering of politics. The first story deals with the initial affirmation of Wright's intellectual career—his experience within the orbit of the American Communist party. The theme of this memoir is that the party has always been more interested in expanding and solidifying its power than in helping Wright, or any other Afro-American, advance. When he first encounters these party organizers, they made him feel that, "Here at least, in the realm of revolutionary expression, Negro experience could find a home, a functioning value and role." (106)[13] Since the John Reed Club's magazine accepted his poems and he became the secretary of his local unit, Wright slowly came to believe that he could devote himself wholeheartedly to the party cause.

Only as he begins to meet more of the party's regulars does he recognize how alien his instincts are to organized radical politics. For instance, a black Communist lets Wright know that his clean shirt and tie, his shined shoes, and his cultivated speech give him the appearance of a petty bourgeois, while a magazine editor tells him that intrinsic quality is not his only criterion in accepting manuscripts. "We want articles about Negroes, but we never see any Negroes. We need your stuff." (108) As Wright becomes even more involved in party activities, he recognizes the party's resemblance to a slavocracy. "Members of the Party do not violate the Party's decisions," a black comrade tells him; and the party takes on the coloring of a slaveholder who regards each black man only as a cog in its cotton-pickin' machine.

The party that uses African-Americans for its own ends also believes, not unlike the Southern slaveholder, that the only good African-American is a docile one. When he finally breaks from the party's orbit, he remembers, "A heavy burden seemed to lift from my shoulders. I was free." (133)

What makes this memoir a transitional work in Wright's intellectual development is the enormous change in his concept of how good and evil function in social reality. In his early fiction, such as *Native Son*, some characters clearly shone as friends of African-Americans, and others were patently his enemies; and Wright's attitudes toward these figures were decisive. In this and his later work, distinctions in Wright's world become less clearly defined.

I remembered the stories in which I had assigned a role of
honor and glory to the Communist Party, and I was glad that
they were down in black and white . . . for I know in my heart
that I should never be able to write that way again, should
never again express such passionate hope, should never again
make so total a commitment of faith. (146)

The novella *The Man Who Lived Underground* represents
Wright's first wholly imaginative attempt, since *Lawd Today*, at
creating a more fluid and ambiguous moral universe. In Wright's
work crimes were once determined by social conditions and,
therefore, as in *Native Son*, sometimes rationalized, but in *The
Man Who Lived Underground* they are acts of accidental impulse.
Where the earlier book saw "reality" in the most ordinary activities, here Wright describes events that are often preposterous,
whose causes are usually mysterious.

A young Afro-American, escaping from the police, jumps
into a manhole to find himself imprisoned in the underground
darkness. The police, it seems, have accused him of murdering
a Mrs. Peabody; whether he did in fact commit the crime we
never know. Sloshing through the slime, he encounters various
alternatives; and unlike the desperate Bigger Thomas, who is
forced to take whatever aid will come to him, Wright's generally
nameless protagonist scans all choices with the cold eye of
a gambler. Death, the eternal escape, is the first alternative
that fate offers to him. Seeing the tiny nude body of a baby
snagged in sewer debris, he contemplates its significance for
himself only to kick it loose from its mooring, propelling it
down the stream.

Through a crack in the wall of an abandoned sewer case, he
peeks into the basement of a black church and surveys Afro-
American religion, which he finds ludicrously unable to cope
with the problems of life:

His first impulse was to laugh, but he checked himself. They
oughtn't to do that, he thought. But he could think of no

reason *why* they should not do it. Just singing with the air
of the sewer blowing in on them. Pain throbbed in his legs
and a deeper pain, induced by the sight of those black people
groveling and begging for something they could never get,
churned in him. (*Right Man*, 23)

He is seized by the desire to shout that their singing is all in
vain, but he squelches that impulse.

Fundamentally, *The Man Who Lived Underground* is, like
Dostoevsky's *Crime and Punishment*, about the perils of the
social-political choice of complete isolation—a kind of emigration
from America which Ralph Ellison in his prophetic 1945 article
on Wright christened "going-underground."[14] Some years before,
James Weldon Johnson, in *Negro Americans, What Now?* (1934),
described it as the ultimate temptation for his people:

> This tendency toward isolation is strong because it springs
> from a deep-seated, natural desire—a desire for respite from
> unremitting, gruelling struggle; for a place in which refuge
> might be taken. We are again and again confronted by this
> question. It is ever present, though often dormant.[15]

Like Dostoevsky before him, Wright meticulously illustrates
how separation from the world slowly debilitates the outcast's
moral character and, eventually, his human essence. First, the
protagonist progressively loses any recognition of how his actions
relate to others, as well as any sense of moral value and any
pragmatic awareness of actual effect. He burrows into a radio
shop and steals some merchandise that he cannot use; and as he
later observes the owner of the shop accusing an employee of
theft, he wonders why he is unable to feel guilty, conjecturing
that the major reason for the absence of feeling is his inability
to relate goods to people. That is, he cannot recognize that he is
taking something from some*body*. In a later scene, after he robs
a safe, he watches the police physically beat its watchman into
making a confession; and to his surprise, he feels little remorse.
In discovering that anything is possible, he makes the collateral

discovery that nothing is morally unjustifiable. "Maybe *any*thing is right he mumbled. Yes, if the world as men have made it was right, then anything else was right, any act a man took to satisfy himself, murder, theft, torture." (47)

Second, as he loses his sense of human values, Wright's protagonist develops a less encumbered, more honest relation with things. After stealing from the bank, he finds himself swamped with $100 bills, watches, and jewels, items of immense value in the society above ground; however, unlike food and clothing and shelter—necessities for the sustenance of the body—these luxuries have no essential value, neither economic nor moral, to a man alone.

> He did not feel that he was stealing, for the cleaver, the radio, the money, and the typewriter were all on the same level of value. . . . They were the serious toys of the men who had lived in the dead world. (40)

Treating the goods as toys, he glues the bills to the walls; he hangs the gold watches on nails driven into the wall. "There was no time for him now." (45)

Upon emerging from the hole into the midst of traffic, he finds that cars swerve "to shun him and the gaping hole," and a voice screams, "You blind, you bastard?" which is to say blind to worldly realities. (54) Soon after, he enters a black church, hoping for solace. His appearance is too fantastic for the environment:

> His cheekbones protruded from a hairy black face; his greasy cap was perched upon his head and his eyes were red and glassy. His shirt and trousers were caked with mud and hung loosely. His hands were gummed with a black stickiness. (55)

As an anonymous voice complains that "he's filthy," an usher escorts him back into the street. Later, he inexplicably goes directly to the police station and confesses to his crime. The policemen reveal that someone else has already confessed to the Peabody murder, and they attempt to dismiss him as a crank. "We don't want you, see? You're free, free as air. Now go home and forget it. It was all a mistake." (60) However, the man who lived underground no longer comprehends the worldly reality of social "freedom"; instead, he insists that the police arrest him and, to clinch their case, accompany him to his cave. Embarrassed, the officers follow the man to his sewer; and once he descends the ladder, they shoot him. The reason for their violence, it is assumed, is that such a free, truth-telling African-American is a real threat to society.

Wright's explanation for this metamorphosis in character resembles Dostoevsky's: Once a man becomes the sole inhabitant of his own universe, he becomes his own God. "Sprawling before him in his mind," Wright says of his protagonist, "was his wife, Mrs. Wooton for whom he worked, the three policemen who had picked him up. . . . He possessed them now more completely than he ever possessed them when he had lived aboveground." (34) Once a man becomes the sole ultimate judge of his actions, he also becomes his own God; anyone so emancipated from extrinsic authority is capable of anything, both crime without guilt and honesty without prudence. The man who lived underground also loses his human identity. When he first steals a typewriter, he picks the name "freddaniels," which may or may not be his own; but once he returns to his cave, he discovers that he has forgotten his name. Earlier, coming upon a lunch basket, he gobbles up the sandwiches and fruit with the greed of an uninhibited animal. "Then, like a dog, he ground the meat bones with his teeth." (30) Wright's final point is that escape into total isolation, while it may at first seem attractive, if not inevitable, condemns the escapee to qualities not fully human.

Soon after *Black Boy*'s publication, Wright himself was foiled in an attempt to buy a safe apartment in Manhattan; and as an invitation from France arrived in this period, he accepted it and soon took a foreign residence that for the rest of his life signified expatriation.[16] After several years abroad, he published

The Outsider, his longest work, a book that also represents his most ambitious attempt to incorporate the insights of European existential philosophy into an understanding of Afro-American experience. In its political references, *The Outsider* recapitulates the major themes of those two transitional works discussed before. From *I Tried To Be a Communist* came Wright's critique of the Communist Party and its relations with Afro-Americans and from *The Man Who Lived Underground* came this critique of the perils of escape and isolation.

In *The Outsider*, Cross Damon, Wright's protagonist, is a postal employee who survives a subway wreck to emerge from the rubble under his own power. Going to a bar for a drink, he discovers that the police have unwittingly listed him as dead. Because his wife wants a divorce and his mistress threatens him with both a paternity suit and prosecution for statutory rape, Damon decides to capitalize on the false report. After accidentally observing his own funeral, he leaves Chicago for New York, where he assumes the identity and the birth certificate of a man recently dead, becomes a social nomad (which is damon spelled backwards), and forges in both senses a new existence for himself.

The book's major theme is that such disaffiliation from society makes a man dangerously irresponsible; it frees his action from the scrutiny of his peers and his mind from any sense of society's censure. Whereas he was once full of repressed aggression, Damon, freed, is able to murder a friend by crashing a bottle over his head and then dropping his body out of a hotel window. His crime inspires feelings quite distant from remorse. "He had done a horrible thing; he had killed so swiftly and brutally that he hardly recognized what he had done as he recalled it to his mind." (101) Damon witnesses a violent fight between a white racist and an arrogant white Communist who had befriended Damon out of political motives. Entering the brawl, Damon first kills the racist and then quite unexpectedly kills the Communist too, making sure that the scene suggests that they killed each other. "He had no plan when he had dealt those blows of death," the book says. "He knew exactly what he had done; he had done it deliberately, even though he had not planned it." (227) Like the man who lived underground, Damon becomes God of his own universe.

> He had assumed the role of the policeman, judge, supreme court and executioner—all in one swift and terrible moment. . . . He had become what he had tried to destroy, had taken on the guise of the monster he had slain. (230–31)

Later, Damon kills another Communist; after that, his inhuman cruelty drives his new girlfriend, the wife of his first Communist victim, to suicide. Damon progresses toward complete nihilism; on his own deathbed, Damon concludes of his career, "Alone man is nothing." (439) This conclusion complements his earlier statement that modern man "is seeking for an organization of his social life." (387) Of the characters in the book, only one survives the chaos, Sarah Hunter, who escapes by rejoining the community of a Catholic church. (434) Finally, the book casts Damon's isolation as a metaphor for all sorts of disaffiliation, including going underground and expatriation.

Wright's critique of the deficiencies of the Communist party has two dimensions—intrinsic, its relations with itself; and extrinsic, its relations with the world, especially Afro-Americans. In the first respect, the party makes its functionaries into rocklike agents of its higher will. "[Damon] could think of no words that he could muster that would convey to Gil [the first Communist victim] the depth of his rejection to him." (117) Elsewhere, Damon was awed by Gil's inhumane machinelike efficiency on behalf of party activities, and later he learns how the party could drive its own members to suicide. The cause of this dehumanization, Damon learns, is that the party demands of its activists such a totality of obedience and commitment that loyalty presumes the suppression of essential human recalcitrance. As one character, Menti, tells Damon, "I've no life except that of the Party. I have no wish, no dream, no will except that of the Party." (279)

The party's major deficiency in dealing with non-Communists
is that it has no awareness of the freedom and fluidity of life.
Early in his experiences with them, Damon discovers that the
freedom of art and intellect are antithetical to the Communist
conception of reality.

> The Communists, instead of shooting the capitalists and bank-
> ers, as they had so ardently swore that they would do when
> they came to power, make instead with blood in their eyes
> straight for the schoolteachers, priests, writers, artists, poets,
> musicians, and the deposed bourgeois governmental rulers as
> the men who held for them the deadliest of threats to their
> keeping and extending their power. (200)

Immediately before this realization of the party's anti-intellectual
animus, Cross Damon "marveled at the astuteness of both Communist and Fascist politicians who had banned the demonic
contagions of jazz," (200) which is to say the spirit of African-
American culture.

Moreover, the experience described in the novel would confirm
District Attorney Houston's remarks that the party was blind
to human reality. (419) Indeed, these remarks echo Wright's
earlier reference to blindness as a metaphor encompassing more
than visual sight. "The Communists were not unintelligent [Cross
thought]. There was one thing of which he was certain: they
would never credit him with as much freedom to act as they had.
A certain psychological blindness seemed to be the hallmark of
all men who had to create their own worlds. . . . All other men
were material for them; they could admit no rivals, no equals."
(269) The politics of *The Outsider*, then, offer no solution, except
for two truths important to Wright: that the Communist party's
interest in Afro-Americans is duplicitous at best and that isolation
from society is the precondition of pathological behavior.

Wright's final novel, *The Long Dream*, recapitulates much
of his previous critique of life in the South, albeit now in
sketchier form; but its end introduces an alternative new in

Wright's fiction—expatriation to Europe. Wright's protagonist is Rex "Fishbelly" Tucker, an Afro-American teenager living in a Mississippi town where his father, a successful undertaker, is a prominent citizen. Despite his family's importance within the Afro-American community, Fish is still at the mercy of white authority; and once they discover that he faints easily when threatened, sadistic whites dub him "the fainting Negro" and frequently subject him to a routine unpleasant to him but comic for them—threatening him with castration until he faints.

The most successful strategy for coping with this imbalance of power is playing dumb before white authority. As Fish's father, Tyree, warns his son:

> I know how to handle these white folks. There ain't *nothing* I couldn't git from 'em if I tried. Son, you just lissen to your papa who brought you into the world and you'll never go wrong. . . . But you got to know *how*! Let me tell you a secret, Fish. A white man always wants to see a black man either crying or grinning. I can't cry, ain't the crying type. So I grin and git anything I want. . . . Fish, the only way to git along with white folks is to grin in their goddam faces and make 'em feel good and then do what the hell you want to behind their goddam backs! (129–30)

Although Fish finds he cannot argue with his father's success, the strategy still repels him as a vulgar compromise with what he feels to be his human dignity. The first time he recognizes his father paying humble deference to a white man, Fish thinks, "This was a father whom he had never known, a father whom he loathed and did not want to know." (115) Later, when his father explains the strategy to him, Fish responds with feelings of rejection; as Wright puts it, "He also discovered that he had no father. He knew in a confused way that no white man would ever need to threaten Tyree with castration; Tyree was already castrated." (132) Like the younger generation in *Uncle Tom's Children*, Fish has higher hopes for his own life.

Still, Fishbelly learns to adopt the duplicitous strategy as his own most effective method for dealing with Southern whites. When, for example, the local sheriff asks Fish if he plans to leave Mississippi, he "lied with as much conviction as he could muster" that life in the South was perfectly suitable. This mode of deference is so deeply ingrained in him that even when he goes North and encounters a seemingly sympathetic white who asks, "How is it down there," Fish replies with a patent lie, "It's awright. We live just like anybody else." (345–46) The major limitation of the strategy is, of course, that at the same time the technique evades the entrenched authority it also implies acceptance of its legitimacy; thus, the Afro-American is always at the mercy of those for whom he plays this role. Southern white authority, in this case, murders Tyree and imprisons young Fishbelly.

A considerably slighter political novel than any of the earlier works, *The Long Dream* does not mention alternatives for the Afro-American in the South; nor does it deal with the possibility of emigration to the North. Rather, expatriation is the only solution offered. At one point, Fishbelly's friend Sam mentions Africa as a possibility:

> "I don't want to go to no Africa," Zeke muttered.
> "Me neither," Tony hissed.
> "Sam wants us to git naked and run wild and eat with our hands and live in mud huts," Zeke ridiculed Sam's thesis. (31–32)

In an elementary form, these young men echo Wright's own opinion, outlined in both *Black Power* (1954) and *White Man, Listen* (1957), that African culture is too primitive for a Western-born black person. Instead of Africa, Fishbelly looked to France, especially after his friend Zeke, stationed with the U.S. Army in Orleans, France, writes home to him, "I'm thinking of settling down for a spell in good ole Paris. Man, it's good to live in this grayness where folks don't look mad at you just because you're black." (329) Once he is released from jail, Fish collects his assets and boards a plane. The novel closes just as he is about to land in France to achieve, the novel suggests, a new, better existence.

During Wright's lifetime, many a commentator pointed out that the novelist was unable to portray Afro-American life in Europe.[17] After Wright's death in 1960, his wife found among his papers five fragments from an unfinished novel, tentatively entitled "Island of Hallucination," which he intended to be a sequel to *The Long Dream*. These fragments were published in 1963 in Herbert Hill's anthology of Afro-American writing, *Soon One Morning*. They deal with Fishbelly's first day in Paris; and although Wright shows through the absence of such incidents that the young Afro-American doesn't suffer from racial prejudice, the episodes largely portray him as lost in an alien culture. In short, while Wright could posit expatriation as the best solution, given the conditions of Afro-American life, he was not yet able to portray convincingly how life in Paris could be better than that in America.[18]

In the end, then, Wright consistently, but unsystematically, undercuts the political alternatives espoused in earlier works. If both *Uncle Tom's Children* and *Black Boy* favored emigration from the South to the North, both *Lawd Today* and *Native Son* showed how dreadful life in Chicago could be for a Southern-born Afro-American. If *Native Son* and, to a lesser extent, *Uncle Tom's Children* dramatized that Communists could be the Afro-American's truest friends among whites, *I Tried To Be a Communist* and *The Outsider* portrayed Communists as exploiters of African-American hopes. If *The Long Dream* implicitly advised a Southern Afro-American to go directly to Europe, bypassing the northern United States, then the unfinished novel portrayed him or her as lost in an alien culture. Elsewhere, the politics implicit in Wright's writing reveals paradoxes verging on contradictions.[19] Religion in, for example, *Lawd Today* is portrayed as an irrelevant panacea, but *The Outsider* describes it as offering some African-Americans a sense of community against the anomie of urban life;

most of Wright's later fiction saw political action within America as ineffectual, but Wright in the earliest fiction recognized the potential power in the mass protest movement within the South— a power realized within his own lifetime; but Wright himself was never again to treat that possibility in his fiction.

His œuvre embodies a series of rejections, first of the American South, then of the Northern cities, then of Communism, then of America itself, then perhaps of expatriation; for Wright's positives grew out of his negatives, his affirmations of the moment out of the rejections of his immediate past, until toward his own premature death he seemed to have no more alternatives to offer. Yet, in pursuing such a torturous path, Wright's fiction seems finally to posit a great political theme, which is the inevitable outcome of his portrayal of the perils of isolation, especially in *The Man Who Lived Underground* and *The Outsider*, and that theme is the meaninglessness of existence in limbo, the utter void of living with no political purpose at all.

NOTES

1. Ralph Ellison, *Shadow and Act* (New York, 1964), 94.

2. Isaac Rosenfeld, *The Age of Enormity* (New York, 1962), 100.

3. Walter Rideout, *The Radical Novel in the United States* (Cambridge, Mass., 1956), 260, 298.

4. For explanations of "signifying," see Roger D. Abrahams, *Deep Down in the Jungle . . .* (Hatboro, Pa., 1964), 54, 267; and Harold Wentworth and Stuart Berg Flexner, *Dictionary of American Slang* (New York, 1960), 477.

5. See Wright, "I Tried To Be a Communist," in Richard Crossman, ed., *The God That Failed* (New York, 1959), 144; Constance Webb, *Richard Wright* (New York, 1968); and Wright, *Black Power* (New York, 1954), xi.

6. Daniel Aaron, *Writers on the Left* (New York, 1965), 397.

7. For the symbolic significance of this scene, I am indebted to Robert A. Bone, *The Negro Novel in America* (New Haven, Conn., 1958), 147.

8. See also Ellison, *Shadow and Act*, 83.

9. Ellison, *Shadow and Act*, 83.

10. Ellison, *Shadow and Act*, 85.

11. Webb, *Richard Wright*, 207, 428.

12. These incidents are repeated in the posthumously published *American Hunger* (1977), which purportedly represents the remainder of *Black Boy*. The later book includes a critique of the Communist Party different from that in *I Tried To Be a Communist* but comes to essentially similar conclusions. *American Hunger* differs from everything else written by Wright prior to 1945 in forecasting emigration at its conclusion (134–35): "Well, what had I got out of living in the city? What had I got out of living in the South? What had I got out of living in America? I paced the floor, knowing that all I possessed were words and a dim knowledge that my country had shown me no examples of how to live a human life."

13. All page numbers refer to the work as printed in Crossman's *The God That Failed*, 1959. Also see Irving Howe and Lewis Coser, *The American Communist Party* (Boston, 1957), 525ff.

14. Ellison, *Shadow and Act*, 94.

15. James Weldon Johnson, *Negro Americans, What Now?* (New York, 1934), 13.

16. Saunders Redding, "A Symposium on an Exiled Native Son," in Herbert Hill, ed., *Anger, and Beyond* (New York, 1966), 205.

17. See, for example, Saunders Redding, "The Alien Land of Richard Wright," in Herbert Hill, *Anger, and Beyond*, 59.

18. For a more extensive plot summary of the entire novel-length manuscript, see Webb, *Richard Wright*, 372–74.

19. For a searching and provocative critique of Wright's ambivalences, see Harold Cruse, *The Crisis of the Negro Intellectual* (New York, 1967), 181ff.

five

Ralph Ellison

Invisible Man is *par excellence* the literary extension of the blues. It was as if Ellison had taken an everyday twelve-bar blues tune (by a man from down South sitting in a manhole up North in New York singing and signifying about how he got there) and scored it for a full orchestra.

—Albert Murray,
"Something Different, Something More" (1966)

In this history of political themes in the Afro-American novel, Ralph Ellison is the natural successor to Richard Wright. Not only were the two men once close friends—indeed, Wright's magazine, *The Negro Quarterly*, was the first to publish Ellison—but one of Ellison's early extended literary essays, "Richard Wright's Blues," published in *Antioch Review* (1945, and quoted before), both comments upon Wright's *Black Boy* and forecasts Ellison's own novel. That is, the essay both clarified his indebtedness to Wright and staked the territory he would pursue. The following quotation from the black writer Albert Murray, also among Ellison's oldest friends, suggestively defines the artistic relationship between the two novelists:

> When Wright encountered [Ellison] shortly after [the essay appeared], all Wright could do was shake his head

in pleased bewilderment—somewhat, one imagines, as the original tunesmith of "Body and Soul" must have done upon meeting Coleman Hawkins—and all he could say was almost exactly what one imagines the tunesmith must have said: "Man, you went further than the book. Much further."

All Ellison, a former trumpet player and student of music composition, could do was shake his head in turn and smile reassuringly and reply, "Well, what you wrote made it possible for me to say what I said about it. All I was trying to do was play a few riffs on your tune. It was your tune. I just hope I didn't embarrass you."[1]

True enough, Ellison's own novel, in many respects, takes off from Wright's work—the younger man plays "a few riffs" on his elder's tunes—for Ellison's narrator undergoes so many of the same experiences that touch Wright's protagonists that *Invisible Man* becomes in many respects an implicit commentary on a predecessor's œuvre. For instance, the narrator of *Invisible Man* is as passive as Bigger Thomas in that both allow things to happen to them, each never realizes his own identity. The crucial differences are that Ellison's narrator is portrayed as self-deceived, while Wright's is not, and that approximately the same range of experience that Wright spreads through several works of fiction is, in *Invisible Man*, compressed into a single novel. Ellison also echoes James Weldon Johnson in his use of an ironic narrator and metaphors for social disengagement. (In fact, his wife Fannie McConnell, while an undergraduate, typed Johnson's autobiography, more than a dozen years before she married Ellison.)

Ellison has defined the central problem for any novelist, whether black or white, as "converting experience into symbolic action."[2] In *Invisible Man*, he creates a nameless narrator whose adventures, always approximate or unspecific in time and place, represent in symbolic form the typical experience of many, if not most, of the active elements—Du Bois's "talented tenth"—of African-American people. As Ellison put it in 1964 in a lecture at the Library of Congress, "It is through the process of making artistic forms . . . that the writer helps give meaning to the experience of the group."[3] In this statement, especially in its tactile imagery, Ellison echoes Stephen Dedalus's ambition, in James Joyce's *Portrait of the Artist as a Young Man*, "to forge in the smithy of my soul the uncreated conscience of my race." In scope as well as detail, he is writing African-American literature. It is indicative that none of the other writers discussed here has his technical capacity for rendering various accents, all of them reflecting differences in geographic background, class, and style.

In the major sequences of *Invisible Man*, the narrator confronts a succession of possible choices for Afro-Americans. When an alternative seems adequate enough to win the narrator's favor, his acceptance becomes, in effect, a pragmatic test of its viability. After he discovers the posited solution is inadequate to his needs, as all of the solutions become, he samples another. Although Ellison's narrator does not confront every known political possibility, the novel is still the most comprehensive one-volume fictional—symbolic—treatment of the history of African-Americans in the twentieth century.

In the opening quarter of the novel, the narrator eagerly tests opportunities for Afro-American existence within the South; and just as Voltaire's Candide innocently embraces the philosophical optimism predominant in his times, so the young black assumes the prevalent notions of the early twentieth century on how black people could best succeed in the South—those of Booker T. Washington. From a vantage point later in time, the narrator remembers that as a young man about to graduate from high school, "I visualized myself as a potential Booker T. Washington," who hoped to follow his idol's advice and perhaps emulate his career. (21) History remembers Washington as having urged his fellow Afro-Americans to lead an honest and industrious life within the Southern framework of segregation—to be a labor force, rather than a political force. The most successful blacks, he believed, were those who proved themselves essential to white society, either because they knew an employable trade or because they helped keep order within the Afro-American community. A general statement of this position is implied in the following passage from *Up from Slavery* (1901):

> The whole future of the Negro rested largely upon the question as to whether or not he should make himself, through his skill, intelligence, and character, of such undeniable value to the community in which he lived that the community could not dispense with his presence.[4]

From this proposition stemmed Washington's major corollary: Since the South offered Afro-Americans greater social and economic opportunities, Afro-Americans of Southern birth would be wise to remain where they were born. "Whatever other sins the South may be called to bear," he wrote, "when it comes to business, pure and simple, it is in the South that the Negro is given a man's chance in the commercial world."[5] At the base of Washington's politics, then, was a trust in Southern whites to give the cooperative black a fair chance to succeed and to honor whatever successes Afro-Americans had achieved for themselves.

From these assumptions, Booker T. Washington, as history and Ellison's narrator saw him, derived three major lines of conduct implemented at his Tuskegee Institute (which resembles the college in *Invisible Man*). First, Washington believed that to make themselves as appealing as possible to white society, Afro-Americans had to be industrious in their work, respectful in their dealings with white superiors, responsible for their families and their communities, and, perhaps most important, scrupulously clean. In *Up from Slavery*, his most influential book, Washington never ceased proclaiming the advantages of an immaculate appearance. For Tuskegee's students, instruction in hygiene was apparently as important as trade- and book-learning:

> It has been interesting to note the effect that the use of the toothbrush has had in bringing about a higher degree

of civilization among the students. With few exceptions, I have noticed that, if we can get a student to the point where, when the first or second toothbrush disappears, he of his own motion buys another, I have not been disappointed in the future of that individual. Absolute cleanliness of the body has been insisted upon from the first. The students have been taught to bathe as regularly as to take their meals. . . . Most of the students came from plantation districts, and often we had to teach them how to sleep at night; that is, whether between the two sheets . . . or under both of them. The importance of the use of the nightgown received the same attention.[6]

Thus, in the daily schedule at Tuskegee, Washington allocated one half hour for cleaning one's room, and school officials made periodic inspection tours of the dormitories. A central aim of Tuskegee's education was to take a back country black and, metaphorically, soak him or her with whitewash.

Second, if an Afro-American is to succeed, he or she must *not* challenge the systems of white supremacy. In Washington's pet epithet, he or she must campaign for "responsibility," not "equality." A demand for equal rights, he feared, could violently disrupt the stability of the South; for not only would revolt have little chance of success, the cost in Afro-American lives would be too exorbitant to make it worthwhile. "The wisest among my race understand that the agitation of questions of social equality is the extremist folly," he wrote, because an Afro-American, following Washington's own example, must "deport himself modestly in regard to political claims."[7] Political rights, he urged, "will be accorded to the Negro by the Southern people themselves, and they will protect him in the exercise of those rights," only if he or she treads the path of humility, impresses white society with his or her conscientiousness, and contributes to its material prosperity.

Third, Afro-Americans must measure success in tokens of recognition from white society, rather than in terms of respect from their own people. This is the major lesson that Washington drew from his own life, and in the latter half of his autobiography he catalogues the honors he received from white America. He especially enjoyed lecturing before groups of white Southerners, and he saved his most important speeches for the racially mixed audiences of large Southern expositions. Among his deepest desires was to have the president of the United States visit Tuskegee; and when the possibility arose, he twice journeyed to Washington, D.C., to persuade McKinley to come. Furthermore, few things pleased him more than encountering a group of white people who, like some Georgia men mentioned in his book, "came up and introduced [themselves] to me and thanked me earnestly for the work that I was trying to do for the whole South."[8] (Whether they addressed him by his Christian name or "Mr. Washington" he does not disclose.) What peers think of an Afro-American's work was not as important as what white folks judged; again, Washington felt that African-Americans could best succeed in America by conforming to the prescriptions of entrenched white authority.

Ellison's narrator so thoroughly and innocently subscribes to the Washingtonian ethic that, when he is selected to give the valedictory address at his segregated high school, he echoes both Washington's ideas and his rhetoric. Telling his black classmates to cultivate friendly relations with their white neighbors, the narrator quotes the key line of Washington's Atlanta Proclamation Address, "Cast down your bucket where you are," (32) for, it is implied, if black Southerners look for water elsewhere they may die of thirst. Likewise, the narrator uses the Washington phrase "social responsibility" (33) to define the Afro-American role in the South. Upon his graduation the narrator believes that he can rise through the Southern system, perhaps becoming, like his idol, an educational leader, or more modestly a doctor or lawyer in the black South.

The narrator, along with other class leaders, is invited to a gathering of local white citizens. At the occasion, they ask the narrator to repeat his valedictory address. When he arrives at the meeting, he is directed to join his classmates in a free-for-all "battle royal" that is one of the features of the evening's entertainment. Although he instinctively shies away from bodily contact with classmates bigger than himself, the narrator, as a Washingtonian, wants to please the white audience and so consents to the ordeal. Along with the other black youths, he is blindfolded with white cloth; once bells sound, he is pushed into the ring. "Everyone fought hysterically," he remembers. "It was complete anarchy. Everybody fought everybody else. No group fought together for long. Two, three, four, fought one, then turned to fight each other, were themselves attacked." (26) Throughout the fight, the white citizens on the sidelines encourage the black boys to "knock" one another's "guts out." This incident, like most of the major scenes in the book, embodies a symbolic dimension that complements the literal action; that is, the scene stands for something larger in the experience of Southern Afro-Americans. Here the novel shows how white powers make Afro-Americans channel their aggressive impulses inward upon their own race instead of upon their true enemies, who remain on the sidelines, supervising the fray to make sure the violence is directed away from themselves. This battle-royal episode also echoes a scene near the end of *Black Boy*, where Wright and another young man get paid to fight one another.[9]

To pay for the "entertainment," the hosts put numerous coins and bills upon a rug and encourage the black teenagers to pick up "all you can grab." Once this new contest starts, the boys discover the rug is electrified. The shocks lead the boys to jump and shriek in animal-like movements, to the amusement of the white audience. "Glistening with sweat like a circus seal and . . . landing flush upon the charged rug," one boy "literally dance[d] upon his back, his elbow beating a frenzied tattoo upon the floor, his muscles twitching like the flesh of a horse stung by many flies." [30] In other words, before an Afro-American in the South receives the pay he has earned, he must overcome unnecessary hazards, often arbitrarily imposed, and publicly make a fool of himself. Between the Afro-American and the money he earns from white Southern society are, symbolically, all the galvanic terrors of an electrified rug, and the price of a white man's pay includes the Afro-American's debasement of his humanity.

After the other boys are paid their pittances and excused, the narrator delivers his speech. Again he voices the platitudes of Booker T. Washington, feigning an air of sincerity with appropriate accents of emphasis. These positive words, however, do not impress the audience. "Still they talked and still they laughed, as though deaf with cotton in dirty ears." (32) When the narrator mentions the phrase "social responsibility," they ask him to repeat it again and again, until in a moment of mental exhaustion he subconsciously substitutes the word "equality." Challenged by the audience, he quickly reverts to the traditional, unrevolutionary phrase. What the novel illustrates here is that as the speaker's censor relaxes, his true desires are revealed; but as soon as he remembers the power of Southern authority, he immediately represses his wish. At the end of the meeting, the superintendent of the local schools presents the narrator with a briefcase; in it is a scholarship to the state college for blacks. Again the political meaning is that an Afro-American must publicly humiliate himself and suppress his true desires before he or she will receive rewards from white Southern society. One problem with Booker T. Washington's guidance is underestimating the real cost of Afro-American success in the South.

In the second sequence of the novel, the narrator discovers what kinds of Afro-Americans receive rewards totally disproportionate to their work. As a student, the narrator is assigned to act as a chauffeur for a white trustee, Mr. Norton, whose name at once echoes "Northern" and Charles Eliot Norton, the first professor of art history at Harvard and heir to a certain kind of New England Brahmin liberalism. Responding to Norton's commands, the narrator drives the old man to the black slum down below the "whitewashed" college on the hill. At his passenger's request, the narrator stops the car before a log cabin belonging to Jim Trueblood, who, as his name suggests, represents the primitive, uneducated Afro-American who is unaffected by the values of white culture. Discovering, to his horror, that Trueblood has impregnated his daughter, Norton asks the black man whether he feels "no inner turmoil, no need to cast out the offending eye?" Refusing Oedipus's response to a similar sin, the black man replies uncomprehendingly, "My eyes is allright," adding, "When I feels po'ly in my gut I takes a little soda and it goes away." (52) Prompted by Norton's queries, Trueblood tells how the officials at the nearby college responded to his misdeed: "The biggity school folks up on the hill . . . offered to send us clean outta the county, pay our way and everything and give me a hundred dollars to git settled with." (51) To the "whitewashed" blacks, Trueblood represents the elemental humanity that the procedures of college education must eliminate, and Trueblood's presence near the campus serves as a reminder of a primitive past the college community wants to repudiate.

To escape their strategy of alternative threats and enticements, Trueblood enlists the aid of his white boss who, in turn, refers him to the local sheriff. That official and his cronies so relish Trueblood's tale of sexual indiscretion that they ask him to repeat all the details, giving him food, drink, and tobacco in return for the voyeuristic pleasure.

> They tell me not to worry, that they were going to send word
> up to the school that I was to stay right where I am. It just
> goes to show yuh that no matter how biggity a nigguh gits,
> the white folks always cut him down. (52)

In the days following, Trueblood becomes a celebrity, attracting the interest of white people he had never encountered before:

> The white folks took to coming out here to see us and talk
> with us. Some of 'em was big white folks, too, from the big
> school 'cross the State. Asked me lots 'bout my folks and
> kids, and wrote it all down in a book. (52)

Presumably these men were Southern scholars who intended to use Trueblood's confessions as evidence of the inherent immorality of Afro-Americans. Moreover, Trueblood reports, local white people now give him more work. "I'm better off than I ever been before," he says. "I done the worse thing a man can do in his family and 'stead of things gittin bad, they got better." (65) In short, Trueblood's experience contradicts Washington's belief that white society would reward only those Afro-Americans who lived by its official morality. Instead, it eagerly appreciates a black man who conforms to the traditional stereotype of an immoral primitive in black skin.

After leaving Trueblood, the narrator follows Norton's command to take him to a roadside bar. Here they encounter a group of hospitalized Afro-American veterans, mostly psychiatric patients, going to the ironically named "Golden Day" for their weekly round of drinks and prostitutes. Their shepherd is the hospital attendant Supercargo who, as his name suggests, functions as their collective superego. Not only does he impose the repressive forces of white society upon them but he also attempts to internalize obedience into their own consciences. Therefore, as soon as he disappears to fetch a drink upstairs, the men "had absolutely no inhibitions." (71) A brawl ensues, directed largely against Supercargo and the social forces he represents. As the "veterans" air their complaints, the narrator discovers that they are brutalized and dispossessed Southern black middle class. One is an ex-surgeon who was dragged from his home by white men and beaten, it is implied, for saving the life of a white person. Another is a composer on the borderline of lunacy, "striking the [piano] keyboard with fists and elbows and filling in other effects in a bass voice that moaned like a bear in agony." A third "was a former chemist who was never seen without his shining Phi Beta Kappa key." (79) The lesson of their experience is that Southern society destroys Afro-American talent and genuine accomplishment. Once again, Washington's advice on how Afro-Americans should live is shown to be an inadequate guide.

Back on the campus, the narrator is summoned into the office of the college president, Mr. Bledsoe. The young man is to be reprimanded for taking Norton down to the slum, for letting him talk to Trueblood, for leading him to the Golden Day, and for allowing the college benefactor to hear complaints from the dispossessed Afro-Americans. The narrator is blamed for innocently following Norton's commands and, even worse, for honestly answering his queries. The heart of the young man's error, Bledsoe says, is that, "You forgot to lie." "But," the narrator replies, "I was only trying to please him." To this excuse Bledsoe retorts in anger, "Why, the dumbest black bastard in the cotton patch knows that the only way to please a white man is to tell him a lie! What kind of education are you getting around here?" (124) The lesson that the young man missed is that one does not necessarily obey a white man; one only seems to do so. Bledsoe believes, echoing cynical implications in Washington's thought, that the black college should preach the attainment not of dignity and self-achievement but of surface obsequiousness and underlying cynicism. Had not, the narrator remembers, Bledsoe himself been a model of such behavior? Had not he illustrated how Afro-Americans should play the role of second-class man:

> Hadn't I seen him approach white visitors too often with his hat in hand, bowing humbly and respectfully? Hadn't he refused to eat in the dining hall with white guests of the school, entering only after they had finished and then refusing to sit down, but remaining standing, his hat in his hand, while he addressed them eloquently, then leaving with a humble bow. (96)

Since Bledsoe's authority within the college is absolute, the narrator willingly accepts punishment for the mistakes his innocence engendered—expulsion. Recognizing that his ethics cannot cope with Southern reality, the young man heads for New York, armed with several of Bledsoe's letters of recommendation.

> How had I come to this? I had kept unswervingly to the path placed before me, had tried to be exactly what I was expected to be, had done exactly what I was expected to do—yet, instead of winning the expected reward, here I was stumbling along.

> . . . For, despite my anguish and anger, I knew of no other
> way of living, nor other forms of success available to such
> as me. (131)

Rather than succumb to the new reality he discovers, the young man who scrupulously followed the suggestions of Booker T. Washington is now forced to disobey his idol's advice and leave the South.

Perhaps the final commentary on Booker T. Washington's politics is the address given in the college chapel by the Reverend Homer Barbee, who is identified as a visitor from Chicago. Barbee presents all the optimistic Washingtonian platitudes, predicting the improvement of conditions in the South and greater opportunity for black people to fulfill their worldly ambitions. Instead of bitterness, emigration, revolt, and racial conflict, Barbee offers the hope of success within the Southern system—a "bright horizon" through self-improvement. As he says, "Great deeds are yet to be performed, for we are a young, though a fast-rising, people. Legends are still to be created." (120) Barbee's ideas have a certain appeal to the narrator and his classmates, until the narrator realizes that the Chicago minister wears dark glasses. He is blind, both in the physical sense and in his awareness of political realities (like Mary Dalton's mother in *Native Son*). To the Afro-American in quest of self-fulfillment, the South in fact offers hope only to the blind, the immoral, and the cynical. This is the political conclusion of the first section of the book.

Before he lets his narrator explore much of Northern life, Ellison introduces a scene that serves as a symbolic portrait of the underlying reality of black-white relations in America. Ostensibly, the chapter describes the operation of a paint factory, but the remark that the factory "looks like a small city" indicates symbolic resonances. (172) The narrator is assigned to mix ten drops of black paint into every can of "Optic White." When he protests that the black would discolor the pure white, his Caucasian foreman replies, "Never mind how it looks. You just do what you're told and don't try to think about it." (175)

Unaware of the physical principle that mixing small amounts of black paint into white paint actually makes white whiter, the narrator scrupulously follows instructions. This process for enriching white paint symbolically parallels the interplay of racial colors in America. The presence of a black minority makes the white world whiter; for since its values and aspirations emulate those of the white world, blacks reinforce the white American way of life. By choosing white modes of behavior, the Afro-American, like the black in the can of paint, embellishes the whiteness of American public life. Likewise, since the paint will be used on a national monument, the passage suggests that all of American history has a similar color composition. The company's motto is, ironically, "Keep America Pure with Liberty Paints." When the narrator inadvertently takes his refill from the wrong tank, the mixture he produces is "not as white and glossy as before; it has a grey tinge." (178) If put on the national monument, it would reveal the heretical truth that American life, underneath the white surface, is like the color grey, indeed a mixture of black and white. For this grievous mistake, the narrator is removed from his paint-mixing job. If he had likewise revealed the actuality beneath the whitewashed surface of America, it is implied, he would have been exiled from the country.

In the second part of the novel, the narrator arrives in New York to test the opportunities open to Afro-Americans in Northern cities. He carries seven sealed letters of introduction from President Bledsoe to philanthropic white liberals who are patrons of the college. At six of the offices, the narrator asks to see the man to whom the letter is addressed. The letter is taken from him and purportedly delivered, and each time the secretary returns and informs the narrator that the important man will contact him later. None fulfill that promise, for unbeknownst to the narrator Bledsoe's letters tell the businessmen that this student has seriously violated some undisclosed rule of the school:

This case represents one of the rare, delicate instances in which one for whom we held great expectations has gone grievously

astray, and who in his fall threatens to upset certain delicate
relationships between certain interested individuals and the
school. (168)

However, in this concluding sentence, Bledsoe, perhaps disin-
genuously, asks each recipient to help the young man. The lesson
portrayed by this episode is that Northern white philanthropists
will aid "Negroes" in the South, but they will not rescue an
individual, needy, Southern black new to the North. They suffer
from hyperopia: pain in the distance can be seen clearly, while
that close at hand is blurred.

Since one of the businessmen is away from New York, the narrator postpones calling at his office. Finally getting an interview,
the narrator meets the son of "Mr. Emerson," by his symbolic
name an heir to the American liberal tradition. This man speaks
in platitudes, often using a second platitude to double back on
the first: "Ambition is a wonderful force," he tells the narrator,
"but sometimes it can be blinding. . . . On the other hand, it can
make you successful—like my father. . . . The only trouble with
ambition is that it sometimes blinds one to realities." (162–63)
He is also extremely self-conscious, if not neurotic. "Don't let
me upset you," he tells the narrator, "I had a difficult session
with my analyst last evening and the slightest thing is apt to set
me off." (163) When he makes a slip of the tongue, Emerson
stops to ponder its significance. He boasts of the number of
Afro-American acquaintances he has—artists and intellectuals
all—and of his regular attendance at an important Afro-American
club. Being, as he says, "incapable of cynicism," he reveals to
the narrator the deceitful contents of Bledsoe's letter. However,
because he is afraid of disobeying his father's wishes, young
Emerson does not hire the narrator and warns him not to reveal
their conversation to anyone. The Northern Emersonian liberal,
according to the novel, is too torn by neurosis, self-doubt, and
compromise to help an Afro-American in need.

Recognizing that those who support him in principle offer few
opportunities in practice, the narrator seeks a job as a laborer at

Liberty Paints. He is hired, he later discovers, as a scab, because the company wants to replace its unionized white workers with cheaper nonunion black labor. A fellow worker tells the narrator of the employer's "racket." "The wise guys are firing the regular guys and putting on you colored college boys. Pretty smart. That way they don't have to pay union wages." (173) The narrator is assigned to the foreman named Kimbro, described as a "slave driver." (174) Assuming this traditional role, Kimbro instructs his Afro-American workers in their jobs. When a worker makes an error, as does the narrator, Kimbro exercises an overseer's authority and assigns him to another task.

After his mistake in mixing colors, the narrator is assigned to assist Lucius Brockway in the third subbasement of the plant. Whereas the workers hired with the narrator represent one type of Afro-American labor—the temporary scabs—Brockway embodies another, less numerous kind. In the words of the critic Robert A. Bone, "[He] represents the skilled stratum of Negro labor which has been entrenched in American industry from the beginning—the black base on which our industrial pyramid is reared."[10] Since Brockway's job is to control and service the machines that mix the base of the paint, the whole operation of paint-making depends literally upon his talents. The company has in the past frequently attempted to replace Brockway with white labor—during Brockway's illness an engineer of Italian ancestry was assigned to the job—but no one else can do his work. Fearing that someone else will intrude on his domain, Brockway is fanatically antiunion. He is entirely subservient to white authority, taking a childish delight in the company's dependence upon him and his special relationship with the boss. Years before, he had helped the "Old Man" make up the slogan, "If It's Optic White, It's the Right White." (190) Also, when Brockway retired, the Old Man discovered the paint's quality was declining and personally persuaded Brockway to return to this job. Underpaid and underpraised, Brockway survives in the industrial system by embracing the existing authority and by having indispensable talents.

One day, the narrator inadvertently enters a union meeting in the locker room. The white workers, assuming that the black man is applying for membership, at once suspect that he is a company spy. One member proposes that the narrator prove his loyalty to the union before he be permitted "to become acquainted with the work of the union and its aims." (194) Although the novel does not develop this encounter, the incident suggests that before the labor movement will accept an Afro-American, he must go to inordinate lengths to justify his right to belong. Once the union people identify him as suspect, they make no effort to ascertain his actual attitudes toward unions. "They had made their decisions without giving me a chance to speak for myself." (195) As the narrator departs, the meeting chairman tells him, "We want you to know that we are only trying to protect ourselves. Some day we hope to have you as a member in good standing." (195)

What is illustrated in the novel is that to both white industry and white unions an Afro-American is acceptable only if he or she is either more loyal or more competent than a comparably qualified white, and employers would in addition prefer that his or her labor be less expensive. "The existence of racial prejudice in both employee and employer groups is of course an indisputable fact," wrote Horace R. Cayton and George S. Mitchell in 1939, in *Black Workers and the New Unions*. "If there were no economic advantages in employing Negroes, most employers would prefer a white labor force."[11]

This situation creates what the sociologist Robert K. Merton christened the self-fulfilling prophecy: "In the beginning, a *fake* definition of the situation [evokes] a new behavior which makes the originally false conception come *true*."[12] If the dominant majority decides that Afro-Americans are unfit to become union members because, it is reasoned, their lower standard of living allows them to take jobs at less than the prevailing wage, then the Afro-Americans, as a result of exclusion, will become strikebreakers, accepting the lower wage and, it follows, necessarily adjusting their lives to the lower standard of living. Similarly, if an employer decides that Afro-Americans are incapable of doing important work, then, acting upon his or her false belief, the employer gives blacks only menial jobs. If an Afro-American, having no other choice, accepts the distasteful labor and handles it competently, then, in the employer's eyes, the Afro-American has "proved" he or she is fit only for menial work. Both employers and unions, then, exploit Afro-Americans' second-class position in American society, and neither offers a suitable solution to their predicament. Later in the novel, a misunderstanding, coupled with a difference in attitude, prompts a fight between the narrator and Brockway. An explosion occurs, and the narrator finds himself in a hospital. Here he undergoes an unidentified operation somewhat resembling a lobotomy, from which, the doctor promises, he will emerge with a "complete change of personality." (206)

In the development of the novel, this chapter and the one following it serve a transitional function; for whereas the narrator once accepted the conventional solutions to the Afro-American dilemma, now he is emancipated from this narrow sense of possibility and prepared to sample more radical alternatives. Upon returning to his boardinghouse, a residence for more ambitious Afro-Americans in New York, he recognizes that his housemates embody the vanities and deceits of those who either failed to climb through the existing system or deluded themselves with artificial tokens of success.

> The moment I entered the bright, buzzing lobby of Men's House I was overcome by a sense of alienation and hostility. My overalls were causing stares and I knew that I could live there no longer, that that phase of my life was past. The lobby was the meeting place for various groups still caught up in the illusions that had just been boomeranged out of my head: college boys working to return to school down south; older advocates of racial progress with utopian schemes for building black business empires; preachers ordained by no authority except their own, without church or congregation, without bread or wine, body or blood; the community "leaders" without followers; old men of sixty or more still caught up in post–Civil War dreams of freedom within segregation; the

> pathetic ones who possessed nothing beyond their dreams of
> being gentlemen, who held small jobs or drew small pensions,
> and all pretending to be engaged in some vast, though obscure,
> enterprise, who affected the pseudo-courtly manners of certain
> Southern congressmen and bowed and nodded as they passed
> like senile old roosters in a barnyard; the younger crowd for
> whom I now felt a contempt such as only a disillusioned
> dreamer feels for those still unaware that they dream—the
> business students from southern colleges, for whom business
> was a vague, abstract game with rules as obsolete as Noah's
> Ark but who yet were drunk on finance. (223)

This critical perception complements the lobotomy; for just as
the narrator assumes a new identity (the operation caused him to
forget his name), so he emerges from his residence hotel with a
different set of inclinations.

Soon after, when the narrator discovers some poor old blacks
being brutally evicted from their flat, he delivers a militant speech
on their behalf. As his efforts attract a Harlem crowd, the narrator
is accosted by a red-bearded man who introduces himself as
"Brother Jack." To overcome the narrator's immediate distrust
of his aggressiveness, Jack ingratiates himself by praising the
narrator's extemporaneous speech: "*History* has been born in
your brain." (253) Jack explains that he belongs to a radical
action group; and once the conversation becomes more relaxed,
the narrator accepts Jack's request to see him in the evening. That
night, the narrator is introduced to the "Brotherhood," quickly
persuaded to become a salaried organizer for the movement, and
assigned to a "theoretician" who will educate him in its aims and
methods. The Brotherhood represents the American Communist
Party in thin fictional disguise.

This third major section of the novel portrays the narrator's
discovery that this radical movement understands neither his
existence nor that of his people. From the opening conversation,
Brother Jack speaks a language strange to the Afro-American
experience. Addressing the narrator as "brother," Jack offers him
cheesecake, a white delicacy largely foreign to Afro-American

taste. Furthermore, he muses on how "history has passed by" the old evicted Afro-Americans who are, he adds, "agrarian types, you know. Being ground up by industrial conditions. Thrown on the dump heaps and cast aside. They're like dead limbs that must be pruned away so that the tree will bear young fruit or the storms of history will blow them away." To this the narrator responds, "Look, I don't know what you're talking about. I've never lived on a farm and I didn't study agriculture." (253) Later with an inappropriateness that is typical of him, Jack predicts that the Brotherhood will transform the narrator into "the new Booker T. Washington." (264) A conciliator like Washington is precisely the opposite of the kind of leader a radical group needs; a reference to, say, Frederick Douglass would have been more appropriate. Moreover, the Brotherhood's images of Afro-Americans come from the storehouse of bourgeois stereotypes. When one "brother" asks the narrator to sing a spiritual, the narrator replies that he cannot sing. The brother's reply is, "Nonsense, *all* colored people sing." (270) Although aware of the Brotherhood's imperviousness, not to mention imperiousness, the narrator is flattered enough to cast his lot with them.

From his earlier contact with the movement, the narrator recognizes that he must assume a precast role. When he accepts the job, he is outfitted with a new identity—on a slip of paper is written his new name. At a Brotherhood party, he overhears a female leader say, "But don't you think he should be a little blacker," and the statement prompts him to think, "What was I, a man or a natural resource?" (263) Later, the Brotherhood suggests that he move to a new address and discontinue writing to his relatives for a while. When Jack introduces him to the larger circle under his new identity, the narrator notices, "Everyone smiled and seemed eager to meet me, as though they all knew the role I was to play." (269) Though the narrator senses that the Brotherhood's aims and methods do not coincide with his own, he accepts the role they thrust upon him for two reasons—because it offers him a key to understanding his experience and "the possibility of being more than a member of a race." (308)

What the narrator fails to see at this point, and discovers later, is that being "more" than a member of his race means being less of an Afro-American. After he joins the Brotherhood, the narrator symbolically attempts to sever connections between himself and his Southern black past. In a boardinghouse in Harlem, he discovers an object embodying much ulterior meaning:

> The cast-iron figure of a very black, red-lipped and wide-mouthed Negro, whose white eyes stared up at me from the floor, his face an enormous grin, his single large black hand held palm up before his chest. It was . . . the kind of bank which, if a coin is placed in the hand and a lever pressed upon the back, will raise its arm and flip the coin into the grinning mouth. (277)

This figurine represents the historical past that the narrator now wants desperately to forget; it has become "a self-mocking image." (277) When the steam pipe in his room emits a clanking sound, the narrator strikes it with "the kinky iron head," (277) cracking the figurine whose parts scatter across the floor. To escape both the landlady's wrath and his own feelings of guilt, the narrator scrapes the parts into the leather briefcase he received from the Southern businessmen, the same briefcase that once carried Bledsoe's disingenuous letters of recommendation. He drops the package in a garbage can outside an old private house, but the building's landlady demands that he retrieve it (and all that its contents symbolize). He protests; but when she threatens to call the police, he digs his hand into the muck (that lies between him and his Afro-American past) and recaptures the load. Two blocks later, he drops it in the heavy snow, only to find a dutiful passerby bringing it back to him. The narrator cannot dispose of the package or the elements of his character symbolized by it until a point near the novel's end. He later acquires from another black brother a link from a work-gang chain that he puts into his pocket; whenever he touches it, the narrator is reminded of his heritage. Through these symbolic devices, the novel makes the point that not even the Brotherhood can separate an Afro-American from his past.

These themes are reinforced by the narrator's introspective monologues. During his affiliation with the Brotherhood, he is haunted by fears of "becoming someone else." Just before he is to deliver his first important speech for the Brotherhood, this man, who never attains a proper name in the course of the novel, feels "with a flash of panic that the moment I walked out upon the platform and opened my mouth I'd be someone else. Not just a nobody with a manufactured name which might have belonged to anyone, or to no one. But another personality." (291) The problem is not that the Brotherhood forces him to do things against his will, but that this new political life is not an organic outgrowth of his own past. His present experience strikes the narrator as a meaningless series of tacked-on events, chance encounters, and sudden fortunes. He becomes aware of two identities within himself:

> The old self that slept a few hours at night and dreamed sometimes of my grandfather and Bledsoe and Brockway and Mary, the self that flew without wings and plunged from great heights; and the new public self that spoke for the Brotherhood and was becoming so much more important than the other that I seemed to run a foot race against myself. (330)

A rigorous Brotherhood schedule prevents the narrator from thinking too much about this split; only when he is transferred to a less demanding job does his divided personality oppress him.

If the Brotherhood has little sense of the needs of an individual Afro-American, it is even less aware of the actualities of Afro-American life. Once the narrator becomes an organizer, he quickly rouses a strong, grass-roots movement in Harlem; he makes speeches at public rallies and regularly visits all the important bars. His extraordinary success makes his more experienced black Brothers jealous, and one, Brother Wrestrum (rest room?), accuses the narrator of individual opportunism and dictatorial aspirations. Although one speech earns applause "like a clap of thunder," the narrator is condemned by his Brotherhood superiors, because his talk was "wild, hysterical, politically irresponsible and dangerous, and worse than that, it was *incorrect!*" (303) The emphasis upon the last word suggests to the narrator that, "The term described the most heinous crime imaginable." They criticize him, he belatedly discovers, for neglecting to include the particular ideology that would organize the needy black audience behind the Brotherhood. To prepare him adequately for future speeches, they assign him to an intensive indoctrination program. It is implied, though not specifically illustrated, that these "correct" ideas and phrases are incapable of moving the Harlem audience. After all, if Jack's favorite clichés sound strange to the semieducated ear of the narrator, they would be more wholly foreign to his audience. Precisely by incorrectly gauging the attitudes of Harlem, the Brotherhood eventually destroys the narrator's usefulness for its cause.

Once cleared of suspicions of both disloyalty and personal opportunism, the narrator returns to Harlem to discover that in his absence his personal following has disintegrated. In a symbolic passage, he enters a bar and addresses two old acquaintances as "brothers." The tall one replies inquisitively, "He is relative of yourn?" His cohort adds, "Shit, he goddam sho ain't no kin of mine!" (366) The first asks the bartender, "We just wanted to know if you could tell us just whose brother this here cat's supposed to be?" (367) As the bartender claims to be the narrator's brother, an argument ensues, the tall man protesting that since the narrator "got the white fever and left" for downtown, revealing that his ultimate loyalties were not to Afro-Americans and Harlem, he was no longer a black "brother." (368) Later, the narrator discovers that in his absence the Brotherhood has abandoned its efforts in Harlem. The work he did and the support he organized have all disappeared, and there seems little likelihood he could retrieve lost ground. His own labor for the Brotherhood, he deduces, accomplished nothing. "No great change has been made." (384)

In one comic interlude, the novel suggests that the Brotherhood suffers because many of its organizers and sympathizers
have motivations quite distant from politics. After he finishes
his speech on the "woman question," the narrator is accosted
by an extremely sensual woman who questions him on "certain
aspects of our ideology." Since the questioning will purportedly
take a while, she invites him up to her apartment. Innocently he
accepts her hospitality. She explains, as he enters her sumptuous
apartment, "You can see, Brother, it is really the spiritual values
of the Brotherhood that interest me." (355) As he answers her
questions, she moves ever closer to him, telling him how he
embodies a "great throbbing vitality." After she seduces him
he condemns her for "confusing the class struggle with the ass
struggle." (302)

The Brotherhood's failure to gauge actual Afro-American
needs lies not so much in the confusion of motives exemplified
by the seductive woman as in the blindness intrinsic in the
movement's approach to reality. The Brotherhood's ideology
contains elements appealing to impoverished blacks, particularly
in offering them equal social rights; yet it shows itself unable
to empathize with peoples' multiple needs and spiritual temper.
The novel explains this last failure in both symbolic and narrative
terms. When the narrator is reprimanded by Brother Jack for
not preaching the correct line at the proper time, the narrator
retorts that Jack, as a white man, cannot know "the political
consciousness of Harlem." (406) Jack insists that the committee
is the ultimate judge of reality and that the narrator is disobeying
its "discipline." The narrator replies that Jack wants to be "the
great white father" of Harlem, "Marse Jack." (409) A fight seems
imminent; but before it starts, Jack snatches his glass eye from
its socket. That eye, Jack explains, was lost in the line of duty—
by implication, in following the "discipline." Nonetheless, the
passage suggests not only that Jack is half-blind to the realities
of Harlem—anyone with only one eye has limited perception—
but also that he is incapable of seeing Harlem *in depth*. The
narrator himself recognizes the second implication: "The meaning

of discipline," he figures, "is sacrifice . . . yes, and blindness."
(411) Once he discovers this failure of perception, the narrator
never again feels total loyalty to the Brotherhood.

Still, he accepts their command to see Hambro, the chief
theoretician, who reveals another reason why the Brotherhood
is oblivious to the needs of Harlem. It has abandoned its drive to
recruit Afro-Americans, because, the narrator is told, its emphasis
has switched from national issues to international ones. When
he asks Hambro, "What's to be done about my district," after
explaining the decline in membership and the threats from the
black nationalists, Hambro authoritatively informs the narrator,
"Your members will have to be sacrificed. We are making
temporary alliances with other political groups and the interests
of one group of brothers must be sacrificed to that of the whole."
(433) When the narrator argues that exploiting black people
is cynical, Hambro replies, in characteristic double-talk, "Not
cynicism—realism. The trick is to take advantage of them in
their own best interests." The narrator asks what justifies the
sacrifice of unwitting people, and Hambro replies "the laws
of reality." (434) Who determines the laws of reality? "The
collective wisdom [of the 'scientists'] of Brotherhood" is the
reply. (437) However, as the narrator perceives, the Brotherhood's
science has little contact with hard reality. All that is known is
ideas about history's movements on the world stage; instead of
trying to see Harlem as an idiosyncratic entity, they see it only
as an interdependent cog in a big machine. To the actual lives and
hopes of Afro-Americans, the scientists are completely blind.

After talking with Hambro, the narrator concludes, "Everywhere I've turned somebody has wanted to sacrifice me for
my good—only *they* were the ones who benefitted." (437) This
recognition prompts the narrator's first general thesis about the
relations of white people with Afro-Americans. Both Hambro and
Jack, he thinks, are incapable of seeing a human essence, either
black or white. They believe that only the political part of a person,
that segment that could serve the interests of the movement, is
worthy of attention; all other problems and aspirations, whether

emotional or physical, are ignored. People could just as well be invisible. "Here I had thought they accepted me," the narrator decides, "because they felt that color made no difference, when in reality it made no difference because they didn't see either color or men." (439) He then recognizes that Jack and Hambro hardly differ from Emerson and Norton. "They were very much the same, each attempting to force his picture of reality upon me and neither giving a hoot in hell for how things looked to me. I was simply a material, a natural resource to be used." As the four white figures blend into one, the narrator discovers the core truth of his relationship with them: "I now recognized my invisibility." (439)

This recognition means that the narrator implicitly accepts the warning that Ras the Exhorter, the black nationalist, proffered to him earlier in the book:

> Why you with these white folks? Why a good boy like you with them? You *my* brother, mahn. Brothers are the same color; how the hell you call them white men *brother*? Shit, mahn. Brothers the same color. We sons of Mama Africa, you done forgot? You black, BLACK! You got *bahd* hair! You got thick *lips*! They say you *stink*! They hate you, mahn. You African. AFRICAN! Why you with them? Leave that shit, mahn. They sell you out. That shit is old-fashioned. They enslave us—you forget that? How can they mean a black man any good? How they going to be your *brother*? (320–22)

Ras's point, that all white men, whether enemy or friend, will use Afro-Americans for their own purposes and finally betray them, is supported by the narrator's own understanding of his experience.

Ras himself represents a political alternative for Afro-Americans, as he stands for those black leaders who have espoused a racism that inverts the Manichean color symbolism traditional to the Christian West. Whereas the Western, which is to say American, mythos makes black synonymous with evil, the black racist makes black the color of all that is good. He attracts support from Afro-Americans by making them proud of their blackness. According to a leading scholar of black nationalism, C. Eric Lincoln:

> All black nationalist movements have in common three characteristics: a disparagement of the white man and his culture, a repudiation of Negro identity and an appropriation of "asiatic" cultural symbols. Within this framework, however, they take shape in a remarkable variety of creeds and organizations.[13]

Although the most prominent black nationalists in the period covered by Ellison's novel were Marcus Garvey and Elijah Muhummad, there is little reason specifically to equate, as some critics have done, Ras the Exhorter with either of these figures. Although Ras is described as having, like Garvey, a West Indian accent (142), he favors resettlement in Abyssinia ("Ras" being the Abyssinian word for prince), whereas Garvey wanted to send Afro-Americans to West Africa.[14] In this respect, one could say that Ras is closer to the historic Noble Drew Ali, the self-styled leader of the "Moors," who designated Morocco in North Africa as a black homeland.[15] Moreover, the West Indian's name and speech evoke the Ras Tafari movements of black West Indians.[16] This multiple reference suggests that Ras, like other important characters in the novel, is conceived as a prototype embodying a range of utopian alternatives that have been espoused by several historical figures; and sure enough, Ras's group embodies all three characteristics that Lincoln enumerates as typical of black nationalist movements.

The narrator never allies himself with Ras; for although he knows that Ras is capable of telling the truth about black relations with whites, the narrator also recognizes that the alternative offered by Ras is unrealistic, which is to say absurd in worldly terms. Ras advocates a massive return to Africa which—given the costs, the lack of inhabitable space, and the difficulties of resettlement—would be too hazardous for a typical African-American.

For the United States, Ras preaches counterviolence, which the narrator discovers is ultimately self-destructive. The Harlem battle waged by Ras is most thoroughly described by an anonymous Afro-American who tells his drinking cronies about the riot he has just witnessed. Through this device, the novel reveals not only the absurdity of the battle itself but also the average Afro-American's bemused view of the fray.

You know that stud Ras the Destroyer? Well, man, *he* was spitting blood. Hell, yes, man, he had him a big black hoss and a fur cap and some kind of old lion skin or something over his shoulders and he was raising hell. Goddam if he wasn't a *sight*, riding up and down on this ole hoss, you know one of the kind that pulls vegetable wagons, and he got him a cowboy saddle and some big spurs. . . .

Hell, yes! Riding up and down the block yelling, "Destroy 'em! Drive 'em out. Burn 'em out! I, Ras, commands you— to destroy them to the last piece of rotten fish!" And 'bout that time some joker with a big ole Georgia voice sticks his head out the window and yells, "Ride 'em, cowboy. Give 'em hell and bananas." And, man, that crazy sonofabitch up there on that hoss, looking like death eating a sandwich, he reaches down and comes up with a forty-five and starts blazing up at that window—and man, talking about cutting out! In a second wasn't nobody left but ole Ras up there on that hoss with that lion skin stretched out behind him. Crazy, man.

When he seen them cops riding up he reached back of his saddle and come up with some kind of old shield. One with a spike in the middle of it. And that ain't all; when he sees the cops he calls to one of his goddam henchmens to hand him up a spear, and a little short guy run out into the street and give him one. You know, one of the kind you see them African guys carrying in the moving pictures. (486–87)

Ras rides hard, "like Earle Sand in the fifth at Jamaica," (487) into the mounted police; and although he manages to knock down two cops with his spear, a third policemen fells him with a bullet.

Meanwhile, the onlookers of Harlem are looting the damaged stores. The political point of this episode is quite clear: To the typical Harlemite, Ras's actions are ludicrously ineffectual; for he is neither prepared for a modern battle nor able to win the support of Afro-American people. Moreover, the violence he initiates in the end causes more deaths among blacks than their white enemies. In this respect, the riot echoes the battle royal fought at the beginning of the novel, for in both scenes Afro-Americans vent their anger against their own people.

Against both Ras and Brother Jack is placed Rinehart, who represents the unfettered possibilities of Harlem life. As Ras's thugs are approaching the narrator, he steps into a drugstore and purchases a quick disguise of dark glasses and a wide-brimmed hat. Advancing down the street, he discovers several passersby mistaking him for a certain "Rinehart." Within moments he discovers that Rinehart must be a desirable lover, a gambler, a numbers runner, a police briber, a male whore, a hipster, a zoot-suiter, and a self-ordained Reverend—"Spiritual Technologist." (417–27) The narrator realizes why Rinehart can fill so many holes, for his new dark glasses reveal Harlem as "a merging fluidity of forms." In contrast to the Brotherhood, and also to Ras, who try to squeeze the world into rigid categories that limit the dimensions of existence, the example of Rinehart suggests that Afro-American life in the North offers anonymity and unforeseen possibility:

> In the South everyone knows you, but coming North was a jump into the unknown. The notion was frightening, for now the world seemed to flow before my eyes. All boundaries down, freedom was not only the recognition of necessity, it was the recognition of possibility. And sitting there trembling I caught a brief glimpse of the possibilities posed by Rinehart's multiple personalities. (431)

This discovery echoes the advice that an unnamed veteran gave the narrator back in the Golden Day: "Be your own father, young man. And remember, the world is possibility if only you'll discover it." (139) After this revelation, the narrator perceives that "Hambro's lawyer's mind was too narrowly logical" to understand Harlem. (432)

After hastily departing from Hambro's apartment, the narrator decides "to do a Rinehart," to approach daily life with the most ironic of strategies. Remembering his childhood, he repeats to himself his grandfather's deathbed advice: "Live with your head in the lion's mouth. I want you to overcome 'em with yesses, undermine 'em with grins, agree 'em to death and destruction, let 'em swoller you till they vomit or bust wide open." (19–20) He decides to master the trick of saying yes and no at the same time, yes to please and no to know. "For now I saw I could agree with Jack without agreeing, and I could tell Harlem to have hope when there was no hope." (438) For his Brotherhood superiors he fabricates reports of a nonexistent growth in membership, and at the next Brotherhood gathering he entices Sybil, the wife of the organization's functionary, to come to his apartment. Although he knows that she sees him as just another hypersexual Afro-American, "expected either to sing 'Old Man River' and just keep rolling along, or do fancy tricks with my muscles," he decides this time to exploit his invisibility. (447) However, when she makes "a modest proposal that I join her in a very revolting ritual," the narrator, sometimes a prig, is repelled by what he interprets as an assault on essences deeper than mere sexuality. So, he spends the evening torn between the impulse to throw her out of his bed and wondering how Rinehart would have handled the disconcerting situation. Though he initiates motions he imagines to be Rinehart's, seducing the woman who calls him "boo'ful," he cannot play the role with the assurance of the master.

This experience with the Brotherhood, along with his recognition of the vanity of Ras's efforts, leads the narrator to a decisive decision: "I knew that it was better to live out one's own absurdity than to die for that of others." (484) Later, he elaborates on the theme:

> I've never been more loved and appreciated than when I tried
> to "justify" and affirm someone's mistaken beliefs; or when
> I've tried to give my friends the incorrect, absurd answers
> they wished to hear. . . . Oh yes, it made them happy and
> it made me sick. So, I became ill of affirmation, of saying
> "yes" against the nay-saying of my stomach—not to mention
> my brain. . . . My problem was that I always tried to go in
> everyone's way but my own. I have also been called one thing
> and then another while no one really wished to hear what I
> called myself. So after years of trying to adopt the opinions
> of others I finally rebelled. (495–96)

In the final sequences of the novel, the narrator confronts the
problem of how to face what he takes to be the absurdity of society. In escaping from the police, he jumps through a manhole into
a bin of coal. Unable to climb out, he experiences a "dark night
of the soul" that includes a nightmare in which Norton, Emerson,
and Jack castrate him of his "illusions." Wading through the
tunnels, he finds a large basement cavern that becomes his underground home; in his own way, he accepts Candide's final dictum,
"that we must cultivate our [own] garden." Whereas Rinehart ex-
ploited absurdity for personal gain, the narrator, as underground
man, accepts, as an expatriate, the condition through his own
nonparticipation. "I hibernated. I got away from it all." (496)

However, this escape, he discovers, is not satisfactory either.
"I couldn't be still even in hibernation," he thinks, "because,
damn it, there's the mind, the *mind*. It wouldn't let me rest."
(496) The narrator's conscience inspires him to write a book that
will explain his experience. "Without the possibility of action"
(501), he reasons, existence becomes meaningless, knowledge
is forgotten, and the capacities to love and care are suppressed.
The narrator achieves what Ellison described in his essay on
Wright as the spirit of the blues: "They at once express both the
agony of life and the possibility of conquering it through sheer
toughness of spirit. They fall short of tragedy only in that they
provide no solution, offer no scapegoat but the self."[17] While
he agrees with the wisdom of Louis Armstrong's song, "Open

the window and let the foul air out," he also believes another song that says, "It was good green corn before the harvest." (502) It is the latter belief that leads him to resolve to "shake off his old skin," to repudiate this form of expatriation, and to seek in the above-ground society an existence that allows him to live primarily for himself. He concludes his story affirming the desire to affirm. "There's a possibility that even an invisible man has a socially responsible role to play" (503) In the context of all of his previous adverse experiences and rejections, this becomes the most positive commitment that Ellison's narrator can justifiably make. Even such a tentative affirmation toward life in America, however, reverses the alternative of expatriation, albeit to different places, established in Du Bois's and Wright's fictions and thus makes *Invisible Man* a radical new development in fiction of the political possibilities for Afro-Americans.

NOTES

1. Albert Murray, "Something Different, Something More," in Herbert Hill, ed., *Anger, and Beyond* (New York, 1966), 129.
2. Ralph Ellison, *Shadow and Act* (New York, 1963), 139.
3. Ellison, *Shadow and Act*, 146.
4. Booker T. Washington, *Up from Slavery* (New York, 1959), 42. What Washington actually believed and said, it should be pointed out, differ somewhat from the ideas generally ascribed to him by both followers and enemies. In fact, he spoke out against the grandfather clause, protested lynching, and urged legal action against discrimination. However, since the narrator of Ellison's novel subscribes as a high school student to the prevailing popular image, my summary necessarily deals with the myth, rather than the fact of Washington.
5. Washington, *Up from Slavery*, 155.
6. Washington, *Up from Slavery*, 123.
7. Washington, *Up from Slavery*, 157, 166.
8. Washington, *Up from Slavery*, 120.
9. Richard Wright, *Black Boy* (New York, 1945), 265.
10. Robert A. Bone, *The Negro Novel in America* (New Haven, 1958), 207.

11. Horace R. Cayton & George S. Mitchell, *Black Workers and the New Unions* (Chapel Hill, N.C., 1939), ix.

12. Robert K. Merton, "The Self-Fulfilling Prophecy," in Paul Bixler, ed., *Antioch Review Anthology* (Cleveland, 1953), 298.

13. C. Eric Lincoln, *The Black Muslims in America* (Boston, 1961), 50.

14. Edmund David Cronon, *Black Moses* (Madison, Wisc., 1955), 126–34.

15. Lincoln, *The Black Muslims*, 51–55.

16. Sheila Patterson, *Dark Strangers* (Harmondsworth, England, 1965), 303–6. See also H. Orlando Patterson, *The Children of Sisyphyus* (Boston, 1965).

17. Ellison, *Shadow and Act*, 94.

six

Conclusion

Man's capacity for justice makes democracy possible, but man's inclination to injustice makes democracy necessary.
　　　　　　　　　　　　　　　—Reinhold Niebuhr[1]

The work of each of these novelists, except for Johnson's, exhibits a development in political reference. If Du Bois's first work envisions the creation of a system of Afro-American cooperatives in the South and his second, the formation of black empire within America allied with colored nations around the world, his later novels posit salvation from Afro-Americans either in Africa itself or in the Communist block of nations, as his own rejection of America became more acute. Of all the writers, Du Bois is the most consistently positive; perhaps because his capacity to persuade, as well as his history of genuine influence upon his readers, predisposed him to offering solutions. Nonetheless, his growing disillusionment with America prevented him from acclaiming a form of uprising he envisioned many years before—born in 1955, with the Montgomery bus boycotts, and matured within Du Bois's own lifetime with the first wave of sit-ins in the early 1960s.

Wright followed in the path of Du Bois, assuming many of the same positions, but at a much faster speed. However, the younger man moved beyond Du Bois in the sense that his own novels reject the Communist party as just another slavocracy, and Wright's views on emigration, either to Africa or Europe, were considerably less decisive than Du Bois's. Although Wright favored African-American expatriation to Europe, both in his life and in his novels, he was deeply aware of the limitations of such escapism, inserting the phrase "alien land" in the dedications to both *The Outsider* and *Eight Men* and portraying the perils of cultural disengagement in his most ambitious novel, *The Outsider*, and in his single most realized fiction, *The Man Who Lived Underground*. Wright represents an extension of Du Bois, for he critically confronts Du Bois's advocacies for Afro-Americans— Communism and expatriation.

Ellison's single novel comments not only upon James Weldon Johnson's ironic narrator but also upon both Wright and Du Bois—as Ellison writes, "My own books . . . would be in themselves, implicitly, criticisms of Wright's."[2] Ellison's narrator follows Richard Wright's initial prescription to migrate North; he joins an equivalent of the Communist party and contemplates escape—not to Europe or Africa, but into an underground cave. Ellison's narrator discovers, as do Wright's characters, first, that the Communist party is not an ally of Afro-Americans and, second, that the "freedom" of disaffiliation is a needlessly limited existence. (Had Ellison written *Invisible Man* after the appearance of *The Outsider*, he might have incorporated the experience of expatriation.) What Ellison's narrator envisions, at the end of *Invisible Man*, is a renewed commitment to testing the possibilities of Afro-American life. As Robert Hemenway prefaced his anthologizing an earlier version of my Ellison chapter:

> The anonymous black narrator of [*Invisible Man*] is offered a
> series of life styles in the form of a succession of masks, all
> designed to delude him into believing that people can identify

his substance when they recognize his mask. Obviously, the masks fail because they deny the reality they conceal—the black self that struggles to asserts its humanity amidst a racist America. The fact about this process that is often overlooked is that the *telling* of his story—from the security of an underground room—enables the hero to end the novel with an affirmation of self; his cognizance that masks must be rejected will enable him to leave the underground for the world.[3]

All these novelists suggest three truths about black politics in America. First, a racially extreme faith will never succeed, not only because, as Myrdal and others points out, the Afro-American minority will never realize its aspirations without the cooperation of the white majority but also because such foreign, exclusive creeds do not mesh with America's pluralistic, inclusive culture.[4] Second, escape of any sort is inadequate because of a peculiar paradox: At the same time that the dominant culture restricts Afro-American opportunities, it also offers, as Ralph Ellison put it, "the broad possibility of personal realization which I see as a saving aspect of American life."[5] Moreover, because America is home and an Afro-American grows up knowing its ways, he is more familiar with its social actualities than an Afro-American immigrant to even such favorable racial climates as, say, France or Sweden. Third, the novelists all suggest that prejudice and discrimination, evil and pernicious as they are, do not *totally* shape one's existence, surely not as predominantly as slavery did before emancipation. Therefore, Afro-Americans today who blame all or even most of their failures in life upon responses to their color are actually escaping from their humanity, particularly the universal capacity to initiate one's troubles. Cross Damon, after all, murders of his own free will; Ellison's narrator allows his naïveté to place him in situations that could only bring him pain; Manuel Mansart freely chooses to stay in the South. Freedom is, after all, the opportunity to decline as well as to achieve, to commit evil as well as to construct good.

The youngest of these novelists, Ralph Ellison, is more hopeful about Afro-American possibilities, and in this respect his sympathies resemble those of most Afro-American novelists younger than himself and therefore epitomize the next development in African-American fiction. Whereas three older writers—Chester Himes (born 1909), William Motley (born 1909), and Jean Toomer (born 1894) all escaped—Himes and Motley becoming expatriates in Paris and Mexico City respectively and Toomer reportedly blending into white society—nearly all the younger writers choose to remain in America; and they portray characters who likewise choose to cope with America. One exception is William Gardner Smith (born 1926), whose *Last of the Conquerors* (1948) is, in Robert A. Bone's summary, "an expatriate novel in the Wright tradition,"[6] and whose later fiction, *The Stone Face* (1963), is a rather inconclusive portrait of a one-eyed Afro-American recently expatriated in Paris. After World War II, Smith himself settled in Paris and later moved, with his European wife, to Ghana. Another exception is William Demby (born 1919), who went to live in Rome soon after publishing *Beetlecreek* (1950), but he has since followed the narrator of his second novel, *The Catacombs* (1965), in returning home to America.

Whatever their differences in style or native politics, the novels of William Melvin Kelly, Julian Mayfield, James Baldwin, John Oliver Killens, John A. Williams, Claude Brown, Paule Marshall, Kristin Hunter, and Le Roi Jones all either neglect or reject both Communism or expatriation as possible alternatives. Similarly, in such symposia as Hoyt Fuller et al., "The Task of the Negro Writer as Artist" (*Negro Digest*, April 1965) or the critical essays collected in Herbert Hill's *Anger, and Beyond* (1966) or the anthology edited by John Hendrik Clarke, *Harlem, U.S.A.* (1964), not once does Communism or expatriation emerge as a possibly viable solution, even though the contributors to all these works are critical of America. Indeed, while Afro-American writers have recently proffered some of the most ferocious condemnations of contemporary America—attacks that ironically often appear in conservative white newspapers and magazines—these same writers choose to stay in an America that so eagerly consumes their critiques.[7]

A final observation of this survey is that the later in history black writers are born, the more free they seem of the pressures that constricted their elders as artists. That is, they exhibit more freedom from excessive preoccupation with the race problem than their predecessors did, more freedom to choose what form their art and thought will take; and this freedom, along with a greater consciousness of the processes of creation, means that younger Afro-American writers, cited in this survey and elsewhere, are generally better artists than their predecessors. Whereas Du Bois as a novelist was essentially an amateur (reserving his professionalism for sociology and polemical essays), James Weldon Johnson seems, in retrospect, something of a dilettante, capable of executing an impressive variety of literary tasks from popular song lyrics to autobiography to fiction with generally high competence; but nothing he wrote ranks as first rate.

In a perceptive essay on Richard Wright, the Afro-American theologian and critic Nathan A. Scott, Jr., once wrote, "It may well be that there was none for whom the reality of [the Afro-American] 'extreme situation' constituted so great a burden." This awareness, Scott continues, shaped Wright's sensibility into an "extremist and melodramatic" cast that he developed after writing *Lawd Today*, with its more fluid conception of reality.[8] From *Uncle Tom's Children* to his final novels, Wright was unable to reject or transcend this restricting mode. "That Mr. Wright should have had his ruling passion," Scott wrote, "is not something that we shall hold against him; . . . what was unfortunate in him was his utter defenselessness before it."[9]

In contrast, Ralph Ellison, a novelist in fuller control of his talents, has escaped, or transcended, what he christens the "jug" of social protest, naturalism, and melodrama for the "world" of more various forms. Indeed, what is true for Ellison also characterizes many talented Afro-American writers younger than himself, whether they be novelists like William Melvin Kelley and Paule Marshall, theologians like Nathan A. Scott, Jr., or music critics like Carmen Moore. After all, whatever deficiencies there are in James Baldwin's novels can hardly be ascribed to race, poverty, lack of social opportunity, negative reception from prejudiced white critics, racial discrimination in the awarding of fellowships, or exclusion from either the mainstream of American culture or the New York literary scene; for Baldwin, from the start of his career, when Wright procured a Eugene Saxon Fellowship for him, has professionally had nothing but extraordinarily good fortune.

In the 1965 *Negro Digest* symposium, William Demby wrote, "American Negro writers are suddenly free from the need to make propaganda, free from the need to protest, free from the need to dramatize sociological theses."[10] A younger woman novelist, Kirsten Hunter added, "He may choose not to be a 'Negro writer'—that is, a writer about Negroes—at all. (I think the freedom to make this choice is, ultimately, one of the freedoms Negroes are presently fighting for.)"[11] In the end, then, these writers' ambitions, along with their novels, serve as evidence of a self-realization that Afro-American intellectuals have always desired.

NOTES

1. Reinhold Niebuhr, *The Children of Light and the Children of Darkness* (New York, 1944), xiii.

2. Ralph Ellison, *Shadow and Act* (New York, 1964), 117.

3. Robert Hemenway, ed., *The Black Novelist* (Columbus, OH, 1970), 89.

4. Gunnar Myrdal, *An American Dilemma* (New York, 1962), 749.

5. Ellison, *Shadow and Act*, 115.

6. Robert A. Bone, *The Negro Novel in America* (New Haven, Conn., 1958), 176.

7. See also Albert L. Murray, "Social Science Fiction in Harlem," *The New Leader*, 44, 2 (January 17, 1966).

8. See especially Richard Wright, *Lawd Today* (New York, 1963), 140–42.

9. Nathan A. Scott, Jr., "No Point of Purchase," *Kenyon Review*, 22 (Spring 1961), 339–40.

10. William Demby, in Hoyt Fuller, ed., "The Task of the Negro Writer as Artist," *Negro Digest*, *14*, 6 (April 1965), 59.

11. Kirsten Hunter, in "The Task of the Negro Writer as Artist," 61.

Appendices to
Du Bois and Ellison

W.E.B. DU BOIS (1968)

Only rare men are so important that their life demands autobiographies, and even fewer live, as well as remain important, so
long that, like William Edward Burghardt Du Bois, their career
occasions not one, not two, but three book-length autobiographies:
Darkwater, published in 1920, when Du Bois was fifty-two; *Dusk
at Dawn*, published exactly two decades later; and the recent *The
Autobiography of W.E.B. Du Bois* (1968) that appears slightly
less than five years after his death, at the age of ninety-five,
in Ghana.

Blessed with exceptional intelligence and abundant determina-
tion, Du Bois was, first of all, perhaps the most important black in
American intellectual history, not only for his sustained influence
on Afro-American thinking about racial and social problems but
also for his pioneering one-man study of *The Philadelphia Negro*
(1899) and such contributions to American historiography as
his equally imposing study *Black Reconstruction* (1935). Very
much a literary person, Du Bois was continually writing—books,
articles, reviews, polemics, editorials, and even poems—about a
spectrum of racial subjects for all sorts of audiences. Writing
became such an instinctive response to his own experience that
even situations that would render most of us speechless, such

as the death of an only son, became occasions for his most
stunning essays.

The Autobiography is largely a personal record, neither modest
nor egotistical, neither too distant nor particularly intimate, of an
extraordinary American career. Born in 1868, in Great Barrington,
Massachusetts, Du Bois had, as he was always reminding us,
French, Dutch, and West Indian ancestry; and not only did his
birthplace contain fewer than a hundred Afro-Americans, but
some of his ancestors had lived as freemen for two hundred
years. Du Bois's father absconded soon after his birth, leaving
his middle-aged mother in charge of her single son. A domestic
for most of her years, she inculcated a sense of "excellence
in accomplishment" that, even though she died just after his
high-school graduation, Du Bois never forgot. Around that time
he prophetically initiated a lifelong custom of annotating his
personal papers.

He went to Fisk University, where he earned money by man-
aging the Jubilee Singers, and then to Harvard, where he became
the first member of his race to earn a doctoral degree; then he
received a fellowship for graduate study in Berlin. Although he
took most of his education among whites, he spent all but one
of his subsequent years in Afro-American institutions, either as a
teacher or an officer of the N.A.A.C.P. that he helped establish.
Its magazine, *Crisis*, which he likewise founded and ran for
most of its years as a personal editorial fief, became his primary
polemical platform. Although he could have been a pioneer in
scholarly sociology or historiography, he succumbed to the racism
of American scholarship, which regarded Afro-American scholars
and Afro-American subjects as particularly suited to each other,
and he willingly confined nearly all of his abundant energies to
what we now call "black studies."

He sustained certain long friendships, particularly with the
black educator John Hope and his white N.A.A.C.P. colleague
Joel Spingarn; yet Du Bois was so much more a man of work than
acquaintance that few other people assume major proportions in
his story. Indeed, this memoir suggests that perhaps he identified

less with Afro-American people, from whom he felt something of an alien distance, than with their struggle against adversity and discrimination, a struggle analogous to his own fight as a brilliant, honest, idealistic, and persevering intellectual.

A very prolific writer, Du Bois was also enough of a hack to lift whole passages verbatim from the earlier memoir, *Dusk at Dawn*. But this new autobiography is in crucial respects a different book. Late in the 1940s, as his intellectual influence suffered a perhaps inevitable decline, Du Bois gravitated toward the Communist party; this explains why certain critical remarks about Communism and Communists that he made in the earlier book are expunged from its successor. In 1950, he accepted the Progressive party's nomination to be their New York candidate for the U.S. Senate. This particular drift was abetted by his marriage in 1951 to the popular biographer Shirley Graham, who collaborated with him in writing *In Battle for Peace* (1952) and is perhaps responsible for the noticeable simplification of his formerly ornate and scholarly prose style.

Much in Du Bois's history from this point becomes rather embarrassing. Largely because the U.S. State Department denied him a passport, his Communist friends around the world were able to portray him as a martyr—a role for which such an indomitable and innately successful figure was distinctly unsuited; yet Du Bois responded by toeing the Communist party line so well that this new book contains a shockingly lame rationalization for the 1956 Soviet repression of Hungary. Once he was allowed a passport, Du Bois, then ninety years old, traveled to the Communist countries, collecting honorary degrees and even a Lenin Peace Prize. And though he previously opposed all movements "back to Africa" and did not visit that continent himself until 1923, when he was fifty-five years old, Du Bois in 1961 accepted Kwame Nkrumah's presidential invitation to settle in Ghana, becoming a carpetbagging eminence in a foreign land and eventually assuming Ghanaian citizenship just before his death. When Nkrumah was deposed, Du Bois's widow hurriedly left the country, reportedly losing the original draft of his autobiography but later salvaging a rough photocopy that became the book.

All this background explains the delay in *The Autobiography*'s appearance, as well as the book's sponsorship by International Publishers, also noted for its editions of Marx, Lenin, and Herbert Aptheker, whose recent writings have all but deified Du Bois. As has happened before, Communists courted and converted a figure whose influence had waned considerably, lending him a devoutly appreciative, though smaller, audience in exchange for deference and eventually membership. Even worse, the youth organization now carrying Du Bois's name has little relation to the history, complexity, and ambiguities of his actual ideas and personal example.

Both his thought and activity were riddled by severe contradictions, which this last autobiography expresses, rather than understands. Over the years, Du Bois espoused two opposed positions, wavering between them—one favoring Afro-American self-segregation from the white community (the idea of a black belt of states that the Communist party adopted in the 1930s), the other favoring the classic N.A.A.C.P. idea of aggressive integration. Thus, Du Bois sometimes stood for cooperation with sympathetic whites; at other times, he suggested that Afro-Americans could create their destinies alone. Behind the first-rate intelligence, whose strengths were mostly literary and scholarly, was a peculiarly opportunistic, second-rate political mind.

More important perhaps, Du Bois was a smallish man who cut a rather aristocratic figure, reportedly never appearing in public without his cane and gloves, always confronting audiences with a prepared text in hand, and asking the world to address him as "Burghardt," rather than the more mundane "Bill" or "Ed." Not only was he too proud to be swayed by the pieties of his following to intentionally commit any act that, for example, might land him in jail, but his well-known theory of "the talented tenth" could be regarded as an egoistic extension of his own uncommon experience and achievement. On the other hand, Du Bois also had enough desire for mass support to let personal pique color his political principles, for example, becoming terribly envious of

Marcus Garvey's influence in the 1920s, even though he never quite realized that his own and the N.A.A.C.P.'s hauteur were in part responsible for Garvey's temporary success. In retrospect, one could conjecture that perhaps Du Bois's personal style kept him from the popular influence that was Martin Luther King's.

The irony is that wavering on self-segregation and aggressive integration still plagues much radical Afro-American thinking and activity, perhaps in part because of Du Bois's immense influence upon the older protest leaders. One might suggest that Du Bois's inability to overcome his own parochialism is somewhat responsible for the intellectual confusions of today. Nonetheless, *The Autobiography of W.E.B. Du Bois* is an important book, informed, like Malcolm X's memoir, by the great American theme of personal possibility and disciplined accomplishment in spite of racial prejudice and social disadvantage. Even though each had opportunities and experiences the other lacked, both Du Bois and Malcolm X were men of words— whose abilities with persuasive language served their activism and bestowed them with power available only to a rare few; both knew how language could persuade an audience, as well as dramatize the integrity and purpose of their own lives.

RALPH ELLISON (1967)

Some of America's great books cross the ocean more quickly than others; some even become acclaimed in England before they are recognized in America. However, no first-class novel of recent years has had such a catfish passage to Europe as Ralph Ellison's *Invisible Man* (1952). It won the National Book Award in 1953, and, in more than one literary sweepstakes, it was subsequently chosen the greatest single American novel of the post–World War II period. Curiously, its climb to eminence has been slower in England. When Gollancz issued it in 1954, *Invisible Man* was respectfully received, but it was long out-of-print there until 1966, when Penguin reissued it as a classic.

It is a picaresque novel, tracing the adventures of a young

Afro-American who rejects the segregated society of the South, only to find poverty and isolation in the North; who rejects his apolitical innocence to join the Communists, only to become disillusioned with them and other radicals; who rejects the terrors of the surface world to hide in an underground cave, only to find that escapism is no solution either. At first reading, the novel seems a catalogue of the adverse experiences that befall an innocent Afro-American, but closer reading suggests that Ellison transcends that sentimental cliché, showing how failures that the narrator blames upon his color actually have more general, more human causes.

At first, too, the novel seems heavily autobiographical—the urgency of its first-person prose, along with the narrator's presumptuousness, evokes this impression; but Ellison's own critical essays, recently collected as *Shadow and Act*, should conclusively dispel this common opinion. They reveal Ellison as a thinker of rigorous intellect and premeditation, whose fictional handiwork is more indebted, for one contrasting instance, to the theories of the American philosopher Kenneth Burke than to the novelist's personal experience. Any reader familiar with Burke can identify how each chapter of *Invisible Man* is structured around the Burkean ritual of purpose, passion, pain, and perception.[1] Deeply literate and very observant, aloof from pat assumptions, Ellison is capable of using ideas without becoming their victim.

This wise intelligence enables him to explain certain previously neglected paradoxes of the Afro-American relation to larger American experience, and makes him ready to debunk any theories whose explanations are demonstrably false and unwilling to let any biases interfere with his perceptions of reality or his mission to write novels. He is, before all else, committed to the truth of things; and in an age in which the successful author from a minority background is quickly transformed into a spokesman for his group (even if he is as unrepresentative as, say, James Baldwin), Ellison refuses to speak for anyone other than himself or to assume any major purposes other than the novelistic one of "converting experience into symbolic action."

His observations on Afro-American life are quite different from what we usually hear; and if I may speak with the personal authority of someone who has lived on the outskirts of Harlem for several years, Ellison utters more truths (and even more important, fewer falsehoods) than any other commentator. His crucial theme is that while discrimination and prejudice are nothing but pernicious and objectionable, they do not totally encumber or pervasively determine Afro-American existence. They are nuisances one learns to bear, rather than debilitating pressures. Thus, to say that such social disadvantages have thoroughly dehumanized Afro-Americans, as some black "experts" do, is to falsely portray Afro-Americans as weaker in morale and culture than they actually are. In contrast to the sociological determinists, Ellison would argue that the most conclusive evidence of Afro-American spirit lies precisely in how much has been created in spite of huge adversity—great music, blues poetry, a protest movement that has won the world's respect, an idiom that has influenced the world's speech, a style of living, and much first-rate literature from Jean Toomer's *Cane* (1923) through Richard Wright's novella *The Man Who Lived Underground* (1944) to Ellison's own *Invisible Man*.

Indeed, the clearest evidence of Afro-American genius is the creation, first, of strategies for coping with adverse situations, such as both the language of "signifying" and a dignified non-violent protest; and second, of art attaining classic expressions of tragic failure and recurring adversity—jazz and the lyrics of the blues. Indeed, Ellison is correct in suggesting that the best Afro-American literature owes more to the tradition of the blues than the other tradition of response to adversity—the stance of protest, so-called. "The blues," Ellison wrote in 1945, "is an impulse to keep the painful details and episodes of a brutal experience alive in one's aching consciousness, to finger its jagged grain, and to transcend it, not by the consolation of philosophy but by squeezing from it a near-tragic, near-comic lyricism. As a form, the blues is an autobiographical chronicle of personal catastrophe expressed lyrically."[2] Needless to say perhaps, this passage implicitly acknowledges *Invisible Man*'s debt to the blues.

Few contemporary writers have fought as strongly as Ellison for the novelist's essential right to be free to do his or her own work, perhaps because as an Afro-American writer he is particularly bombarded with prescriptions for how to make himself more "useful" to his race and society. The strength of his professional commitment is especially evident in "The World and the Jug," which is his response to an earlier essay by post-Trotskyist critic Irving Howe, who argued that, because Afro-American life is so oppressively terrible, the only true role for the Afro-American writer is that of creating protest literature, designed to offend white society and goad it into positive social action. Richard Wright becomes the model Afro-American writer in Howe's polemic; and James Baldwin, after rejecting Wright's stance some fifteen years later, had by 1963, with *The Fire Next Time*, come to emulate him. Howe also hinted that Ellison, by not becoming a protest author, indulged some undefined sort of esthetic escapism.

Ellison's essay is as devastating and eloquent a response to normative, bullying, busybody criticism as we have in our time, an uncompromising assertion of the writer's demand for a right to the "world" of free choice of subject and purpose, rather than the imprisoning "jug" of protest literature. Precisely this freedom from social constraint and coercion is what the freedom movement intends to attain. This essay incorporates a subtle analysis of how passionate political commitment can destroy a critic's ability to read clearly, to examine carefully the possible effects of his own position, and to observe the ineluctable realities of existence. Take, for instance, Howe's suggestions that Wright was Ellison's intellectual father—a tactic that Ellison dubs the "Northern white liberal version of the white Southern myth of absolute separation of the races." He continues, "Two days after arriving in New York I was to read Malraux's *Man's Fate* and *Days of Wrath*, and after these how could I be impressed by Wright as an ideological novelist?"[3] (Perhaps Ellison is too modest to suggest a reverse influence; Wright's *The Outsider* can be read as a commentary on *Invisible Man*, published a few years before.) This is one of the few ostensibly personal debates in which real issues are discussed, not careers and personalities, and one of the even fewer that are personally instructive, for this is scarcely the only context in which covert enemies come masquerading as friends.

In addition, *Shadow and Act* contains some extremely intelligent essays on blues and jazz, an insightful study of the similarities between black archetypes and American traditions ("Change the Joke and Slip the Yoke"), some perceptive literary essays on Richard Wright, Stephen Crane, and images of blacks in modern American fiction. Ellison also reprints three literary interviews that shall be important as long as *Invisible Man* is read, and that will be a long time indeed. In its mythic resonance, its complex political truths, its imaginative energy, the wit of its prose, its narrative drive, *Invisible Man* has lasting qualities that successfully combine the virtues of both Faulkner and Dostoevsky. Through the "process of making artistic forms," Ellison says, "The writer helps give meaning to the experience of the group,"[4] and the particular achievement of *Invisible Man* is that it not only speaks for Afro-Americans but that, in the novel's final words, "on the lower frequencies, I speak for you."

Over the past dozen years, sections of Ellison's forthcoming novel have appeared in American literary magazines (*Noble Savage, Quarterly Review of Literature, Partisan Review*), and I have heard him declaim other parts at public readings. As these segments range from impressive to brilliant in quality, few novels in our time have been more eagerly awaited.

NOTES

1. For an introduction to Burkean theories, see Richard Kostelanetz, "Kenneth Burke," in *The New Poetries and Some Olds* (Carbondale, Ill., 1991).

2. Ralph Ellison, *Shadow and Act* (New York, 1963), 78.

3. Ellison, *Shadow and Act*, 118.

4. Ellison, *Shadow and Act*, 146.

Bibliography

For if the word has the potency to revive and make us free, it also has the power to blind, imprison and destroy.
—Ralph Ellison, *Shadow and Act* (1964)

PRIMARY SOURCES

Du Bois, W.E.B. *Dark Princess.* New York: Harcourt Brace, 1928.
———. *Mansart Builds a School.* New York: Mainstream, 1959.
———. *The Ordeal of Mansart.* New York: Mainstream, 1957.
———. *The Quest of the Silver Fleece.* Chicago: McClurg, 1911.
———. *Worlds of Color.* New York: Mainstream, 1961.
Ellison, Ralph. *Invisible Man* (1952). New York: Signet, 1960.
Johnson, James Weldon. *The Autobiography of an Ex-Colored Man* (1912). New York: Hill & Wang, 1960.
Wright, Ellen, and Michel Fabre, eds. *Richard Wright Reader.* New York: Harper & Row, 1978.
Wright, Richard. *American Hunger.* Ed. by Michel Fabre. New York: Harper & Row, 1977.
———. *Black Boy.* New York: Harper, 1945.
———. *Eight Men* (1961). New York: Avon, n.d.

————. "I Tried To Be a Communist" (1944), in Richard Crossman, ed., *The God That Failed*. New York: Bantam, 1959.

————. *Lawd Today*. New York: Walker, 1963.

————. *The Long Dream*. New York: Ace, 1958.

————. *Native Son* (1940). New York: Harper & Row, 1957.

————. *The Outsider* (1935). New York: Perennial Library, 1965.

————. *Uncle Tom's Children* (1938). New York: Signet, 1947.

SECONDARY SOURCES—EXPOSITION

Abrahams, Roger D. *Deep Down in the Jungle . . . .* Hatboro, Pa.: Folklore Associates, 1964.

Andrews, William L., ed. *Critical Essays on W.E.B. Du Bois*. Boston: Hall, 1985.

Aptheker, Herbert. *American Negro Slave Revolts*. New York: Columbia University Press, 1943.

————, ed. *A Documentary History of the Negro People in the United States*. 2 vols. New York: Citadel, 1962, 1964.

Baldwin, James. *The Fire Next Time*. New York: Dial, 1963.

————. *Go Tell It on the Mountain*. New York: Grosset & Dunlap, 1953.

————. *Nobody Knows My Name*. New York: Dial, 1961.

————. *Notes of a Native Son*. Boston: Beacon, 1955.

Bardolph, Richard. *The Negro Vanguard*. New York: Vintage, 1961.

Baumbach, Jonathan. *The Landscape of Nightmare*. New York: New York University Press, 1965.

Bennett, Lerone, Jr. *Before the Mayflower*. Chicago: Johnson, 1962.

————. *Confrontation: Black and White*. Chicago: Johnson, 1965.

————. *The Negro Mood*. New York: Ballantine, 1965.

Benston, Kimberly, ed. *Speaking for You*. Washington, D.C.: Howard University Press, 1987.

Berlin, Isaiah. *The Hedgehog and the Fox*. New York: Mentor, 1957.

Blotner, Joseph. *The Modern American Political Novel, 1900–1960*. Austin: University of Texas Press, 1966.

Bone, Robert A. *The Negro Novel in America*. New Haven, Conn.: Yale University Press, 1958.

Bontemps, Arna, and Jack Conroy. *They Seek a City*. Garden City, N.Y.: Doubleday, Doran, 1945.

Breit, Harvey. *The Writer Observed*. New York: Collier, 1961.

Broderick, Francis L. *W.E.B. Du Bois: Negro Leader in a Time of Crisis*. Stanford, Calif.: Stanford University Press, 1959.

Brossard, Chandler, ed. *The Scene Before You*. New York: Rinehart, 1955.

Brown, Deming. *Soviet Attitudes Toward American Writing*. Princeton, N.J.: Princeton University Press, 1962.

Brown, Sterling, Arthur P. Davis, and Ulysses Lee, eds. *The Negro Caravan*. New York: Dryden, 1941.

Buck, Paul H. *The Road to Reunion*. New York: Vintage, 1959.

Butcher, Margaret Just. *The Negro in American Culture*. New York: Mentor, 1957.

Cable, George Washington. *The Negro Question*. Garden City, N.Y.: Doubleday Anchor, 1958.

Carmichael, Stokely, and Charles V. Hamilton. *Black Power*. New York: Vintage, 1967.

Cash, W. J. *The Mind of the South*. New York: Vintage, 1960.

Cayton, Horace R., and George S. Mitchell. *Black Workers and the New Unions*. Chapel Hill: University of North Carolina Press, 1939.

Chapman, Abraham, ed. *Black Voices*. New York: Signet, 1968.

Clark, Elmer T. *The Small Sects in America*. Rev. ed. New York: Abington, 1949.

Clarke, John Hendrick, ed. *Harlem, U.S.A.* Berlin: Seven Seas, 1964.

Collingwood, Robin G. *The Idea of History*. New York: Oxford University Press, 1956.

Cooper, Wayne, ed. *The Passion of Claude McKay*. New York: Schocken, 1973.

Courlander, Harold. *Negro Folk Song, U.S.A.* New York: Columbia University Press, 1963.

Cronon, Edmund David. *Black Moses*. Madison: University of Wisconsin Press, 1955.

Cruse, Harold. *The Crisis of the Negro Intellectual*. New York: Morrow, 1967.

Davis, Charles T. *Black Is the Color of the Cosmos*. Ed. by Henry Louis Gates, Jr. New York: Garland, 1982.

Dollard, John. *Caste and Class in a Southern Town*. Garden City, N.Y.: Doubleday Anchor, 1957.

Douglass, Frederick. *Life and Times: The Complete Autobiography*

(1882). New York: Collier, 1962.

Drake, St. Clair and Horace R. Cayton, *Black Metropolis* (1945). Revised and enlarged ed. Two volumes. New York: Harper & Row, 1962.

Du Bois, W.E.B. *The Autobiography of W.E.B. Du Bois.* New York: International, 1968.

———. *Black Reconstruction in America, 1860–1880* (1935). New York: Meridian, 1964.

———. *Darkwater.* New York: Harcourt Brace, 1920.

———. *Dusk at Dawn.* New York: Harcourt Brace, 1940.

———. *In Battle for Peace.* New York: Masses & Mainstream, 1952.

———. "A Litany at Atlanta" (1906), *ABC of Color.* Berlin, DDR: Seven Seas, 1964.

———. *The Philadelphia Negro* (1899). New York: Schocken, 1968.

———. *The Souls of Black Folk.* Greenwich, Conn.: Fawcett, 1961.

———. *The World and Africa.* Enlarged ed. New York: International, 1965.

East, Edward M. *Mankind at the Crossroads.* New York: Scribner's, 1923.

Elkins, Stanley. *Slavery.* New York: Grossett & Dunlap, 1963.

Ellison, Ralph. *Going to the Territory.* New York: Random House, 1986.

———. *Shadow and Act.* New York: Random House, 1964.

Emanuel, James A., and Theodore L. Gross, eds. *Dark Symphony: Negro Literature in America.* New York: Free Press, 1968.

Essien-Udom, E. U. *Black Nationalism.* New York: Dell, 1964.

Farr, Finis. *Black Champion.* London: Macmillan, 1964.

Fisher, Miles Mark. *Negro Slave Songs in the United States.* New York: Citadel, 1963.

Foner, Philip S. *Frederick Douglass.* New York: Citadel, 1964.

Forten, Charlotte L. *A Free Negro in the Slave Era.* New York: Collier, 1961.

Franklin, John Hope. *From Slavery to Freedom.* New York: Knopf, 1962.

———. *Reconstruction After the Civil War.* Chicago: University of Chicago, 1962.

Frazier, E. Franklin. *Black Bourgeoisie.* New York: Collier, 1962.

———. *The Negro in the United States.* Rev. ed. New York: Macmillan, 1957.

Gayle, Addison. *Richard Wright: Ordeal of a Native Son.* New York: Doubleday, 1980.

———. *The Way of the New World.* New York: Doubleday, 1975.

———, ed. *The Black Aesthetic.* New York: Doubleday, 1971.

Glazer, Nathan. *The Social Bases of American Communism.* New York: Harcourt Brace, 1961.

———, and Daniel Patrick Moynihan. *Beyond the Melting Pot.* Cambridge, Mass.: M.I.T. Press, 1963.

Gloster, Hugh M. *Negro Voices in American Fiction.* Chapel Hill: University of North Carolina Press, 1948.

Graubard, Stephen R., ed. *The Negro American.* Cambridge, Mass.: American Academy of Arts and Sciences Press, 1965.

Guttmann, Allen. "Focus on Ralph Ellison's *Invisible Man,*" in David Madden, ed., *American Dreams, American Nightmares.* Carbondale: Southern Illinois University Press, 1970.

Handlin, Oscar. *The Newcomers.* Garden City: Doubleday Anchor, 1959.

———. *Race and Nationality in American Life.* Garden City: Doubleday Anchor, 1957.

Harper, Michael S., and Robert B. Stepto, eds. *A Chant of Saints.* Urbana: University of Illinois Press, 1979.

Harrington, Michael. *The Other America.* Harmondsworth, England: Penguin, 1963.

Hassan, Ihab H. *Radical Innocence.* Princeton, N.J.: Princeton University Press, 1961.

Hemenway, Robert, ed. *The Black Novelist.* Colombus, OH: Charles R. Merrill, 1970.

Hentoff, Nat. *The Jazz Life.* London: Davies, 1962.

———. *The New Equality.* New York: Viking, 1964.

———, and Albert McCarthy, eds. *Jazz.* New York: Rinehart, 1959.

Hersey, John, ed. *Ralph Ellison, a Collection of Essays.* Englewood Cliffs, N.J.: Prentice-Hall, 1970.

Hill, Herbert, ed. *Anger, and Beyond.* New York: Harper & Row, 1966.

———. *Soon One Morning.* New York: Knopf, 1963.

Howe, Irving. *Politics and the Novel.* New York: Horizon, 1957.

———. *A World More Attractive.* New York: Horizon, 1963.

———, and Lewis Coser. *The American Communist Party.* Boston: Beacon, 1957.

Huggins, Nathan Irvin. *Harlem Renaissance*. New York: Oxford University Press, 1971.

Hughes, Carl Milton. *The Negro Novelist*. New York: Citadel, 1953.

Hyman, Stanley Edgar. *The Promised End*. New York: World, 1963.

——. "Richard Wright Appraised," in Phoebe Pettingell, ed., *The Critic's Credentials*. New York: Atheneum, 1978.

——. *Standards*. New York: Horizon, 1965.

——. *The Tangled Bank*. New York: Atheneum, 1962.

Isaacs, Harold R. *The New World of Negro Americans*. New York: Day, 1963.

Johnson, James Weldon. *Along the Way*. New York: Viking, 1933.

——. *Black Manhattan*. New York: Knopf, 1930.

——. *Negro Americans, What Now?* New York: Viking, 1934.

——, ed. *The Book of American Negro Poetry*. New York: Harcourt Brace, 1922.

Kardiner, Abram, and Lionel Ovesey. *The Mark of Oppression*. New York: Norton, 1951.

Kazin, Alfred. *On Native Grounds*. Garden City, N.J.: Doubleday Anchor, 1956.

King, Martin Luther, Jr. *Stride Toward Freedom*. New York: Harper & Bros., 1958.

——. *Where Do We Go from Here, Chaos or Community?* New York: Harper & Row, 1967.

——. *Why We Can't Wait*. New York: Signet, 1964.

Kostelanetz, Richard. *Master Minds*. New York: Macmillan, 1969.

Lawrence, D. H. *Studies in Classic American Literature*. New York: Viking, 1964.

Levy, Eugene. *James Weldon Johnson*. Chicago: University of Chicago Press, 1973.

Lincoln, C. Eric. *The Black Muslims in America*. Boston: Beacon, 1961.

Locke, Alain, ed. *The New Negro*. New York: Boni, 1925.

Logan, Rayford W. *The Betrayal of the Negro*. New York: Collier, 1965.

——, ed. *W.E.B. Du Bois: A Profile*. New York: Hill & Wang, 1970.

Lomax, Louis E. *The Negro Revolt*. New York: Signet, 1963.

——. *When the Word Was Given*. Cleveland: World, 1963.

Louis, Joe. *My Life Story*. New York: Duell, Sloan and Pearce, 1947.

Lukacs, Georg. *The Historical Novel*. Boston: Beacon, 1963.

Mannheim, Karl. *Ideology and Utopia.* New York: Harvest, n.d.

Margolies, Edward. *Native Sons.* Philadelphia: Lippincott, 1968.

McCall, Dan. *The Example of Richard Wright.* New York: Harcourt, Brace and World, 1969.

Meier, August. *Negro Thought in America: 1880–1915.* Ann Arbor: University of Michigan Press, 1963.

Murray, Albert. *The Omni-Americans.* New York: Outerbridge & Dienstfrey, 1970.

Myrdal, Gunnar. *An American Dream.* New York: McGraw-Hill, 1964.

Nadel, Alan. *Invisible Criticism.* Iowa City: University of Iowa Press, 1988.

Neff, Emery. *The Poetry of History.* New York: Columbia University Press, 1947.

Newton, Francis. *The Jazz Scene.* Harmondsworth, England: Penguin, 1961.

Niebuhr, Reinhold. *The Children of Light and the Children of Darkness.* New York: Scribner's, 1944.

———. *The Irony of American History.* New York: Scribner's, 1952.

Nordholt, J. W. Schulte. *The People That Walk in Darkness.* New York: Ballantine, 1960.

O'Meally, Robert G. *The Craft of Ralph Ellison.* Cambridge, Mass.: Harvard University Press, 1980.

Oliver, Paul. *Conversations with the Blues.* New York: Horizon, 1965.

———. *The Meaning of the Blues.* New York: Collier, 1963.

Osofsky, Gilbert. *Harlem: The Making of the Ghetto.* New York: Harper & Row, 1966.

Quarles, Benjamin. *The Negro in the Making of America.* New York: Collier, 1964.

Pease, William H., and Jane H. Pease. *Black Utopia.* Madison: State Historical Society of Wisconsin, 1963.

Record, Wilson. *The Negro and the Communist Party.* Chapel Hill: University of North Carolina Press, 1951.

Redding, Saunders. *The Lonesome Road.* Garden City, N.Y.: Doubleday Dolphin, 1958.

———. *On Being Negro in America.* New York: Charter, 1962.

Richmond, Anthony M. *The Colour Problem.* Harmondsworth, England: Penguin, 1955.

Rideout, Walter B. *The Radical Novel in the United States.* Cambridge, Mass.: Harvard University Press, 1956.

Robeson, Paul. *Here I Stand* (1958). Boston: Beacon, 1970.

Rose, Willie Lee. *Rehearsal for Reconstruction*. Indianapolis, Ind.: Merrill, 1964.

Rosenblatt, Roger. *Black Fiction*. Cambridge, Mass.: Harvard University Press, 1974.

Rosenfeld, Isaac. *The Age of Enormity*. New York: World, 1962.

Rourke, Constance. *American Humor*. Garden City, N.Y.: Doubleday Anchor, n.d.

Rudwick, Elliott M. *W.E.B. Du Bois: A Study in Minority Group Leadership*. Philadelphia: University of Pennsylvania Press, 1960.

Schiener, Seth M. *Negro Mecca*. New York: New York University, 1965.

Seton, Marie. *Paul Robeson*. London: Dobson, 1958.

Shapiro, Nat, and Nat Hentoff, eds. *Hear Me Talkin' to Ya*. Harmondsworth, England: Penguin, 1962.

————. *The Jazz Makers*. New York: Holt, Rinehart & Winston, 1957.

Smith, Homer. *Black Man in Red Russia*. Chicago: Johnson, 1964.

Stearns, Marshall. *The Story of Jazz*. New York: Signet, 1958.

Tannenbaum, Frank. *Slave and Citizen*. New York: Vintage, 1963.

Trimmer, Joseph E., ed. *A Casebook on Ralph Ellison's Invisible Man*. New York: Crowell, 1972.

Warren, Robert Penn. *Who Speaks for the Negro?* New York: Random House, 1965.

Washington, Booker T. *Up from Slavery* (1901). New York: Bantam, 1959.

Webb, Constance. *Richard Wright*. New York: Putnam's, 1968.

Wentworth, Harold, and Stuart Berg Flexner. *Dictionary of American Slang*. New York: Crowell, 1960.

Williams, Martin, ed. *The Art of Jazz*. New York: Grove, 1960.

Wilson, Edmund. *To the Finland Station* (1940). Garden City, N.Y.: Doubleday Anchor.

Wilson, James Q. *Negro Politics*. New York: Free Press, 1965.

Woodward, C. Vann. *The Strange Career of Jim Crow*. 2nd Rev. ed. New York: Oxford University Press, 1966.

Wright, Richard. *Black Power*. New York: Harper & Row, 1954.

————. *The Color Curtain*. New York: Harper & Row, 1956.

————. *Pagan Spain*. New York: Harper & Row, 1957.

————. *12 Million Black Voices*. New York: Viking, 1941.

————. *White Man, Listen.* Garden City, N.Y.: Doubleday Anchor, 1957.

X, Malcolm, with Alex Haley. *The Autobiography of Malcolm X.* New York: Grove, 1965.

————. *Malcolm X Speaks: Selected Speeches and Statements.* New York: Merit, 1965.

Zinn, Howard. *SNCC: The New Abolitionists.* Boston: Beacon, 1964.

SECONDARY SOURCES—FICTION

Baldwin, James. *Another Country.* New York: Dial, 1962.

————. *Giovanni's Room.* New York: Dial, 1956.

————. *Go Tell It on the Mountain.* New York: Knopf, 1953.

————. *Tell Me How Long the Train's Been Gone.* New York: Dial, 1968.

Bontemps, Arna. *Black Thunder.* Berlin, DDR: Seven Seas, 1964.

Brown, Claude. *Manchild in the Promised Land.* New York: Macmillan, 1965.

Brown, William Wells. *Clotel, or the President's Daughter.* London: Partridge & Oakey, 1853.

Carew, Jan. *The Last Barbarian.* London: Secker & Warburg, 1961.

Chesnutt, Charles. *The House Behind the Cedars.* Boston: Houghton Mifflin, 1900.

Clarke, John Hendrik, ed. *America Negro Short Stories.* New York: Hill & Wang, 1967.

Demby, William. *Beetlecreek.* New York: Rinehart, 1950.

————. *The Catacombs.* New York: Pantheon, 1965.

Ellison, Ralph. "Flying Home," in Edwin Seaver, ed., *Cross-Section.* New York: Fischer, 1944.

Fauset, Jesse. *Plumb Bun.* New York: Frederick A. Stokes, 1928.

————. *There Is Confusion.* New York: Boni and Liveright, 1924.

Fisher, Rudolph. *The Walls of Jericho* (1928). New York: Arno, 1969.

Griffin, John Howard. *Black Like Me.* New York: Signet, 1961.

Himes, Chester B. *The Big Gold Dream.* New York: Avon, 1960.

————. *If He Hollers Let Him Go.* New York: Doubleday, 1945.

Hughes, Langston, ed. *The Best Short Stories by Negro Writers.* Boston: Little, Brown, 1967.

Hunter, Kristen. *God Bless the Child.* New York: Scribner's, 1964.

————. *The Landlord.* New York: Scribner's, 1966.

Kelley, William Melvin. *Dancers on the Shore*. New York: Doubleday, 1964.

———. *dem*. New York: Doubleday, 1967.

———. *A Different Drummer*. New York: Doubleday, 1962.

———. *A Drop of Patience*. New York: Doubleday, 1965.

Killens, John Oliver. *And Then We Heard the Thunder*. New York: Knopf, 1963.

Larsen, Nella. *Quicksand*. New York: Knopf, 1928.

Marshall, Paule. *Brown Girl, Brownstones*. New York: Random House, 1959.

———. *Soul Clap Hands and Sing* (1961). London: Allen, 1962.

Mayfield, Julian. *The Grand Parade*. New York: Vanguard, 1961.

———. *The Hit*. New York: Vanguard, 1957.

Motley, Willard. *Knock on Any Door*. New York: Appleton-Century-Crofts, 1947.

———. *Let No Man Write My Epitath*. New York: Random House, 1958.

———. *We Fished All Night*. New York: Appleton-Century-Crofts, 1951.

Patterson, H. Orlando. *The Children of Sisyphus*. Boston: Houghton Mifflin, 1965.

Petry, Ann. *Country Place*. Boston: Houghton Mifflin, 1947.

———. *The Street*. Boston: Houghton Mifflin, 1946.

Schuyler, George. *Black No More*. New York: Macauley, 1931.

Smith, William Gardner. *Last of the Conquerors*. New York: Farrar, Straus & Giroux, 1948.

———. *The Stone Face*. New York: Farrar, Straus & Giroux, 1963.

Toomer, Jean. *Cane* (1923). New York: Harper & Row, 1969.

White, Walter. *Flight*. New York: Grosset and Dunlap, 1926.

Williams, John A. *The Angry Ones*. New York: Ace, 1960.

———. *Night Song*. New York: Dell, 1964.

———. *Sissie*. New York: Farrar, Straus & Giroux, 1963.

Wright, Richard. *Savage Holiday* (1954). New York: Award, 1965.

ARTICLES AND ESSAYS

Dickey, James. "Notes on the Decline of Outrage," in Louis D. Rubin and Robert D. Jacobs, eds., *South*. Garden City: Doubleday Dolphin, 1961.

Du Bois, W.E.B. "The Negro and Socialism," in Helen Alfred, ed., *Toward a Socialist America*. New York: Peace Publications, 1958.

Ellison, Ralph. "The Invisible Man," *Horizon*, 93–94 (October 1947).

————. "Society, Morality, and the Novel," in Granville Hicks, ed., *The Living Novel*. New York: Macmillan, 1957.

Feldman, Irving. "Keeping Cool," *Commentary*, 36 (September 1963).

Fleming, Walter L. " 'Pap' Singleton, the Moses of the Colored Exodus," *American Journal of Sociology*, 15 (July 1909).

Franklin, John Hope. "Introduction," *Three Negro Classics*. New York: Avon, 1965.

Fuller, Hoyt, ed. "The Task of the Negro Writer as Artist: A Symposium," *Negro Digest*, 14, 6 (April 1965).

Hyman, Stanley Edgar. "Those Trans-Atlantic Blues," *The New Leader*, 44, 35 (October 16, 1961).

Isaacs, Harold R. "Integration and the Negro Mood," *Commentary*, 34 (December 1962).

Kostelanetz, Richard. "An Interview with Ralph Ellison (1965)," *Iowa Review*, 19, 3 (Fall 1989).

Lynd, Staughton. "The New Negro Radicalism," *Commentary*, 36 (September 1963).

Martin, Kenneth K. "Richard Wright and the Negro Revolt," *Negro Digest*, 14, 6 (April 1965).

Mayfield, Julian. "Challenge to Negro Leadership," *Commentary*, 31 (April 1961).

————, et al. "The Young Radicals: A Symposium," *Dissent*, 9, 2 (Spring 1962).

Merton, Robert K. "The Self-Fulfilling Prophecy," in Paul Bixler, ed., *Antioch Review Anthology*. Cleveland: World, 1953.

Murray, Albert L. "Social Science Fiction in Harlem," *The New Leader*, 44, 2 (January 17, 1966).

————. "White Man's Harlem," *The New Leader*, 47, 25 (December 7, 1964).

Record, Wilson. "Extremist Movements Among American Negroes," *Phylon*, 17, 1 (1956).

Redding, Saunders. "The Negro Writer and His Relationship to His Roots," in Abraham Chapman, ed., *Black Voices*. New York: Signet, 1968.

Rovit, Earl H. "Ralph Ellison and the American Comic Tradition," in Joseph J. Waldmeir, ed., *Recent American Fiction*. Boston: Houghton Mifflin, 1963.

Rowan, Carl T. "Has Paul Robeson Betrayed the Negro?" *Ebony*, *12* (October 1957).

Scott, Nathan A., Jr. "No Point of Purchase," *Kenyon Review*, *23* (Spring 1961).

————. "Search for Beliefs: Richard Wright," *University of Kansas City Review* (Autumn–Winter 1956).

Smith, William Gardner. "Black Man in Europe," *Holiday*, *37* (January 1965).

White, Walter. "Why I Remain a Negro," *Saturday Review Reader*. New York: Bantam, 1951.

Wolfe, Bernard. "Uncle Remus and the Malevolent Rabbitt," *Commentary*, *3* (July 1949).

Wright, Richard. "Two Letters to Dorothy Norman," in William Wasserstrom, ed., *Civil Liberties and the Arts*. Syracuse, N.Y.: Syracuse University Press, 1964.

————. "Urban Misery in an American City," "A World View of the American Negro," *Twice a Year*, *14–15* (Fall–Winter 1946–47).

Index

About the Author

RICHARD KOSTELANETZ, following his tenure as Fulbright Scholar at King's College, University of London, has published numerous books of poetry, fiction, criticism, and cultural history. He has also edited more than two dozen anthologies of art, literature, and criticism. His essays have been published in several periodicals and his visual art, audiotapes, videotapes, films, and holograms have been exhibited and broadcasted internationally. Among his current projects are books about the art of radio in North America, an "ABC of Contemporary Reading," and the maturity of American thought from 1945 to 1967.

OTHER WORKS BY
RICHARD KOSTELANETZ

Books Authored: *The Theatre of Mixed Means* (1968), *Master Minds* (1969), *Visual Language* (1970), *In the Beginning* (1971), *The End of Intelligent Writing* (1974), *I Articulations/Short Fictions* (1974), *Recyclings*, (Volume One, 1974), *Openings & Closings* (1975), *Portraits from Memory* (1975), *Constructs* (1975), *Numbers: Poems & Stories* (1975), *Modulations* (1975), *Extrapolate* (1975), *Come Here* (1975), *Illuminations* (1977), *One Night Stood* (1977), *Tabula Rasa* (1978), *Inexistences* (1978), *Wordsand* (1978), *Constructs Two* (1978), *"The End" Appendix/ "The End" Essentials* (1979), *Twenties in the Sixties* (1979), *And So Forth* (1979), *More Short Fictions* (1980), *Metamorphosis in the Arts* (1980), *The Old Poetries and the New* (1981), *Reincarnations* (1981), *Autobiographies* (1981), *Arenas/Fields/Pitches/Turfs* (1982), *Epiphanies* (1983), *American Imaginations* (1983), *Recyclings* (1984), *Autobiographien New York Berlin* (1986), *The Old Fictions and the New* (1987), *Prose Pieces/Aftertexts* (1987), *The Grants-Fix* (1987), *Conversing with Cage* (1988), *On Innovative Music(ian)s* (1989), *The New Poetries and Some Olds* (1991)

Books Edited: *On Contemporary Literature* (1964, 1969), *Twelve from the Sixties* (1967), *The Young American Writers* (1967), *Beyond Left & Right: Radical Thought for Our Times* (1968), *Possibilities of Poetry* (1970), *Imaged Words & Worded Images* (1970), *Moholy-Nagy* (1970), *John Cage* (1970, 1991), *Social Speculations* (1971), *Human Alternatives* (1971), *Future's Fictions* (1971), *Seeing Through Shuck* (1972), *In Youth* (1972), *Breakthrough Fictioneers* (1973), *The Edge of Adaptation* (1973), *Essaying Essays* (1975), *Language & Structure* (1975), *Younger Critics in North America* (1976), *Esthetics Contemporary* (1978, 1989), *Assembling Assembling* (1978), *Visual Literature Criticism* (1979), *Text-Sound Texts* (1980), *The Yale Gertrude Stein* (1980), *Scenarios* (1980), *Aural Literature Criticism* (1981), *The Literature of SoHo* (1981), *American Writing Today* (1981, 1989), *The Avant-Garde Tradition in Literature* (1982), *Gertrude Stein Advanced* (1990)

Books Co-Authored and Edited: *The New American Arts* (1965)

Books Co-compiled and Introduced: *Assembling* (Twelve Volumes, 1970–1981)

Performance Scripts: *Epiphanies* (1980), *Seductions* (1986)

Portfolios of Prints: *Numbers One* (1974), *Word Prints* (1975)

Audiotapes: "Experimental Prose" (1976), "Openings & Closings" (1976), "Foreshortenings & Other Stories" (1977), "Praying to the Lord" (1977, 1981), "Asdescent/Anacatabasis" (1978), "Invocations" (1981), "Seductions" (1981), "The Gospels/Die Evangelien" (1982), "Relationships" (1983), "The Eight Nights of Hanukah" (1983), "Two German Hörspiel" (1983), "New York City" (1984), "A Special Time" (1985), "Le Bateau Ivre/The Drunken Boat" (1986), "Resumé" (1988), "Onomatopoeia" (1988), "Carnival of the Animals" (1988), "Americas' Game" (1988), "Epiphanies" (1982–), "More or Less" (1988–)

Extended Radio Features: "Audio Art" (1978), "Text-Sound in North America" (1981), "Hörspiel USA: Radio Comedy" (1983), "Glenn Gould as a Radio Artist" (1983), "Audio Writing" (1984), "Audio Comedy Made in America Today" (1986), "New York City Radio" (1987), "Orson Welles as an Audio Artist" (1988), "Schallplatten Hörspiel" (1989)

Videotapes: *Three Prose Pieces* (1975), *Openings & Closings* (1975), *Declaration of Independence* (1979), *Epiphanies* (1980), *Partitions* (1986), *Video Writing* (1987), *Home Movies Reconsidered* (1987), *Two Erotic Videotapes* (1988), *Americas' Game* (1988), *Invocations* (1988), *The Gospels Abridged* (1988), *Kinetic Writing* (1989), *Video Strings* (1989)

Films Produced and Directed: *Epiphanies* (in German, 1983; in English, 1981–)

Films Co-produced and Directed: *Constructivist Fictions* (1978), *Ein Verlorenes Berlin* (1983), *Ett Forlorat Berlin* (1984), *A Berlin Lost* (1985), *Berlin Perdu* (1986), *El Berlin Perdida* (1987), *Berlin Sche-Einena Jother* (1988)

Holograms: *On Holography* (1978), *Antitheses* (1985), *Hollog/rap/her* (1987), *Hollog/rap/hy* (1987), *Abracadabra* (1987), *Lilith* (1987), *Madam/Adam* (1987), *Ambiguities* (1987)

Retrospective Exhibitions: *Wordsand* (1978)

DATE DUE

JAN 1 6 1995			
MY 2 8 '98			
MAR 2 2 1999			
JUN - 1 2000			
DEC - 9 2000			
MAR 2 0 2001			